EVOLUTION OF MODERN POPULAR MUSIC
A history of Blues, Jazz, Country, R&B, Rock and Rap

MARK VINET

North Amer

WWW.I

D1354414

6240

National Library of Canada Cataloguing in Publication

Vinet, Mark, 1964-
        Evolution of modern popular music: a history of blues, jazz, country, R&B, rock and rap / Mark Vinet.

Includes bibliographical references and index.

ISBN 0-9688320-2-4

1. Popular music–20th century–History and criticism.   2. Popular music–19th century–History and criticism.   3. Popular music–United States–History and criticism.   4. Popular music–Canada–History and criticism. I. Title.

ML3476.V783 2004   781.64'09   C2004-900277-5

Artwork: www.proudproductions.com

For any additional information contact:

Mark Vinet
WADEM PUBLISHING
North American Historical Institute / Music History Association
117 Bellevue Street
Vaudreuil-sur-le-Lac, Quebec, Canada, J7V-8P3
Telephone: 450-510-1102 / 450-371-1803
Fax: 450-510-1095
E-mail: mark@markvinet.com
Website: **www.markvinet.com**

AUTHOR

Historian and author Mark Vinet was born in 1964 in Sorel, Quebec, Canada. He is a fluently bilingual (English-French) entertainment and copyright lawyer, and, co-founder and former Executive Vice-President of MPV Entertainment (Kafka Records, Polliwog Festival, artist management, music publishing, music e-commerce, recipient of several ADISQ Félix awards, MIMI awards and JUNO nominations). Recipient of the "James McGill University Entrance Award" he obtained his law degree at McGill, was admitted to the Quebec Bar, and did post-graduate research work in the United States and Europe. Over the past 25 years, Mark has been involved in most aspects of the entertainment business in Canada, USA, and Europe (music, film, television, concerts, Internet). He began his career in music as a recording artist with Capitol/EMI and then switched to the business side of the entertainment industry while living in Los Angeles. He presently teaches college level courses in music history, entertainment business, contracts and copyright law. He currently is the host of an FM radio program and practices entertainment law in Montreal.

Mark Vinet is founder of the Music History Association and the North American Historical Institute, which presents a series of his music history and North American history lectures. He is author of the book entitled *CANADA AND THE AMERICAN CIVIL WAR: Prelude To War* and the French language Civil War book entitled *Le Québec/Canada et la Guerre de Sécession Américaine: 1861-1865*.

DEDICATION

This book is dedicated to my parents. My mother Judith, from whom I acquired my musicianship and appreciation for music, and, my father Claude, who encouraged me to be disciplined, diligent, respectful, fair, and honest in my dealing as an attorney and entrepreneur in the music business. Their example, influence, and steady presence have contributed immeasurably to my success as an artist and businessman in the music industry. Their care, concern, friendship, support, and love shall always be greatly treasured.

ACKNOWLEDGMENTS

I wish to thank the many musicians, authors, scholars, curators, and friends who helped me with my research for this book. My gratitude is extended to all those who warmly greeted and assisted me on my numerous field and research trips throughout North America and Europe.

Louis Armstrong

CONTENTS

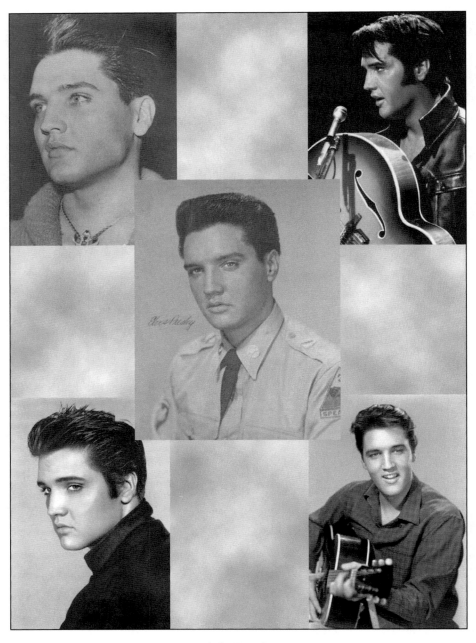

Elvis Presley

LIST OF PHOTOGRAPHS

8

The Beatles

James Brown

Michael Jackson

Madonna

INTRODUCTION

To be on the cutting edge of the music and entertainment industry, one should possess an in-depth knowledge of the evolution of modern popular music, as well as its history, roots, and traditions. Music lovers of all ages will enjoy this engaging overview of pop music from its historic roots to today's chart topping styles. Discover how the changes in recording technology have influenced the music we buy and listen to. Experience a wonderful and fascinating musical odyssey while exploring dozens of idioms including blues, folk, ragtime, jazz, big band, spirituals, blue grass, Tejano, Cajun, musical comedy, western, gospel, country, skiffle, rock and roll, R&B, soul, funk, Motown, hard rock, disco, heavy metal, reggae, corporate rock, punk, worldbeat, new wave, grunge, new age, easy listening, techno, rap and hip hop. A spotlight shines on hundreds of influential artists, songwriters, performers, and music legends such as Louis Armstrong, Robert Johnson, Bing Crosby, Irving Berlin, Duke Ellington, Muddy Waters, Benny Goodman, Frank Sinatra, Miles Davis, Elvis Presley, John Coltrane, Johnny Cash, Bob Dylan, Beatles, Rolling Stones, Joni Mitchell, B.B. King, Neil Young, Paul Simon, Led Zeppelin, Bob Marley, Black Sabbath, Pink Floyd, Bee Gees, Bruce Springsteen, Michael Jackson, Prince, Madonna, Nirvana, Garth Brooks, Metallica, Shania Twain, U2, Celine Dion, and Eminem.

EVOLUTION OF MODERN POPULAR MUSIC is the first in a series of books dealing with the history of music by author, musician, entertainment lawyer, and historian Mark Vinet. It offers an in-depth study and detailed analysis of the dramatic events and talented individuals who created and later influenced the eclectic, vibrant, and colorful art form known as pop music.

To better appreciate the contents of this book, certain specific terminology and abbreviations should be noted. For example, the term "North America" refers principally to the countries of Canada and the United States. World War One (1914-18) is abbreviated to "WWI", World War Two (1939-45) becomes "WWII", and "aka" means "also known as". Although some terminology and abbreviations are standard, others are custom-made and delivered by the author. The author believes that voluntary and conscious unorthodox use of the written language for the purpose of effect or emphasis is refreshing and stimulating.

The author has conscientiously chosen to employ capital letters, Italics, and punctuation marks to better present, organize, or emphasize certain passages of this book. Although the standard rules of spelling and grammar are not always voluntarily followed, one hopes this good faith explanation will merit a benevolent acceptance and appreciation from you the reader. This book's detailed Index section omits the word "the" when classifying artist names. For example, the "Beatles" will be indexed under the letter "B".

The author's goal was to make this book enjoyable to write and read, or in other words – a book written to be read. To this end, the author elected to write a book he himself would take pleasure in reading. He strongly believes that history should be savored and enjoyed by all, not only academics, scholars, and historians. Small print and distracting footnotes have been avoided in order to make this book "reader friendly". Although this work is presented without footnotes, it is based on documentation. Any general reader interested in discovering primary and secondary background materials, notes, and sources should locate, without difficulty, the references in the Bibliography. These references should also provide any knowledgeable scholar with the sources that substantiate the context.

The Bibliography lists the references drawn upon for the subject of this book but not its general background. The Bibliography therefore does not list every publication (book, pamphlet, essay, article, diary, letter etc.) and audio/video support (vinyl record, audio cassette, compact disc, VHS cassette, CD-Rom, DVD, etc.) that was utilized by the author relating to the subject's general historical period.

It should be noted that the author attempted to touch upon, cover, or describe as many international musical styles, idioms, and trends as possible. However, in order to best relate the subject, the author chose to place special emphasis on English language and instrumental popular music. Also, the primary focus is on the evolution of modern popular music within a North American context. To this end an entire chapter has been dedicated to Canadian pop music. The author felt most comfortable with this approach and regrets any type of world music not adequately described. In addition, the author asks forgiveness for omitting any particular artist, performer, or musician dear to the reader's heart. It is virtually impossible to mention, illustrate, or portray in detail the multitude of talented individuals who contributed in different ways to the evolution of modern popular music. This book provides the reader with a general overview of the topic at hand.

Finally, this work does not do justice to all the important and often fascinating music industry pioneers, builders, entrepreneurs, innovators, technicians, and inventors who helped transform, deliver, and package pop music into a commercial product, produced and marketed on a mass-commodity basis, and sold to a broad audience. This popular art form would not have flourished without their business acumen, labor, dedication, and accomplishments.

POSTSCRIPT

The author wishes to pay homage to the many associations, organizations, and medical researchers dedicated to the understanding, educating, informing, researching, rehabilitating, and curing of hearing disorders. Musicians, in particular, should better appreciate the miracle of hearing; it being one of the delicate human senses that must be protected and cherished. Please visit **www.markvinet.com** for links and information on this topic.

Led Zeppelin

The Bee Gees

PROLOGUE

Generally speaking, music that is enjoyed by the largest possible audiences is called popular music. Modern popular music is music created as a commercial product of an industry devoted entirely to its manufacture and sale. Types of popular music or "pop" music are numerous and should be divided into styles, idioms, trends, or categories. Within each category, many subcategories may exist. Popular music also includes songs from films, television and musical theatre. Since its beginnings, modern popular music has branched out into so many styles that no single description fits all of them with total accuracy. A few generalizations, however, can be made, keeping in mind that for all of them, exceptions can be cited.

There are many different styles of popular music. In some cases, the categories overlap. For example, jazz and country music evolved out of folk traditions. Some idioms, such as blues and bluegrass, exist both as pop music and as folk music. Also, many classical composers have written pieces in the style of popular music. Pop music is usually distinguished from classical and folk music. Classical music is written chiefly for concerts, operas, and ballets, while folk music is the traditional music of a particular group or community of people. Folk music is the music of ordinary people expressed in songs and tunes that are passed on from one person to another by ear and memory rather than by print, and thus acquire variations. They are sung or played for pleasure rather than for profit, and usually the composer is unknown. For example, the largest number of Anglo-North American folk songs came to this continent with the early settlers from the British Isles and were passed from generation to generation over the last three centuries. Folk music has become a major influence and phenomenon of modern popular music.

While there has been a popular music as long as humans have turned to singing and dancing for diversion and recreation, much of it was folk music and existed only as an oral tradition. But pop music in the modern sense originated in the late 1700s, when ballads made popular in dance music and ballad opera received wide circulation. Distinctive North American styles of pop music emerged in the mid-1800s. Early in the twentieth century, the novelty of infectious jazz rhythms and dominance of woodwind, brass, and percussion instruments over strings attracted some serious composers who occasionally incorporated suitable jazz styles into their works. Since 1930, the influence has worked in both directions, and pop music has gradually adopted techniques that originated in serious music. Regardless of the interaction of pop and serious music, the popularity of the former is one of the most significant musical developments of the twentieth century, especially in view of the widening gulf between the serious composer and the potential audience.

Early musical genres were very influential in shaping modern pop music. Jazz, the quintessential American art form, is a mixture of elements from African folk music and European classical music. The music called jazz drew on ragtime, blues, spirituals, and band music, establishing the melting-pot principle that would see it take in many other cultural influences and musical styles in the following century. Jazz was born in New Orleans but brought up in New York and Chicago. Its evolution has been the result of both personal initiatives and popular movements.

Country and western music roots lie in the British folk tradition, particularly as preserved in the rural mountain areas of the southern United States. The roots of rock music are buried deep in the musical traditions of the blues, jazz, and country styles. Some believe rock music appeals to the teenager in some of us, while jazz appeals to the adult in us all.

The advances in electronics and technology resulted in the tremendous growth of pop music during the twentieth century. New techniques made possible the high-fidelity reproduction of sound and its widespread and rapid mass media dissemination through phonograph records, radio, and television. In addition, some of the instruments used in pop music incorporated electronic amplification as well as sound production. Important shifts in pop music after WWII were tied to social and technological changes. The so-called "Great Migration" of Southern musicians and audiences to urban areas and the introduction of the electric guitar were particularly influential. The history of popular music during the second half of the twentieth century has been dominated by rock music, which, with its variants, including disco, punk, heavy metal, and rap music, spread throughout the world and became the standard musical idiom for young people in many countries.

Although there have been important changes in the technology used to produce popular music, some of the features of pop music have altered relatively little. Most North American pop music still draws upon aspects of popular song forms and the crooning vocal style of the 1920s Tin Pan Alley. It draws as well from the backbeats, call-and-response textures, strong grooves, and emotional intensity of black American music, and the poetic themes and ballad forms of Anglo-American music. Although music idioms, recording artists, and hit songs change constantly, deep continuities remain within North American popular music.

Shaped by economic, social, and technological forces, popular music is closely linked to the social identity of its performers and audiences. Although much pop music expresses romantic sentiments, other pop songs serve as a vehicle for social and political commentary. Although popular music is sometimes thought to have meaning only for the time in which it was created, many pop songs have endured for decades and continue to have relevance and credibility.

The major influence of black musical culture on modern popular music cannot be understated. The various idioms of popular music have followed a path that originated in the mid-1800s with music from minstrel shows. A cycle typically starts when black Americans develop a musical style that is an integral part of a much larger African American subculture, embracing language, fashion, demeanor, and lifestyle\ From the start of this development, a few white Americans become interested in both the music and the subculture and actively participate on the edges of the emerging subculture. Eventually, some of these white participants begin to make their own renditions of the music, some of which then gain popularity among the white youth majority. The popularity of the music transfers part of the language, dance-style, fashion, and attitude of the subculture into the mainstream of North American culture.

The most recent genre of popular music is rap. The advent of rap in many ways parallels the birth of rock and roll in the mid-1950s. Both originated and incubated within the black American community and both were initially recorded by small, independent record companies and promoted to an African American audience. In both cases, the new style gradually attracted white artists, a few of whom began performing it. For rock and roll it was a white American from the South, Elvis Presley, who reached the pop music charts. For rap it was a white band from New York, the Beastie Boys. Their 1986 track *You Gotta Fight for Your Right To Party!*, was one of the first two rap records to reach the top ten list of pop hits. The other important early rap recording to break into the top ten, 1986's *Walk This Way*, was a collaboration of the black rap group Run-DMC and the white rock group Aerosmith.

The unending struggle between the propensity of the music industry to centralize music and the stylistic diversity of musicians continues in the popular music of the twenty-first century. The history of North American pop music may be viewed as a relationship between a mainstream nucleus, located since the late 1800s in New York City, and, later in Nashville and Los Angeles, and various marginal sectors, located throughout the USA and outside the mainstream of the music industry. Whereas the mainstream music industry reproduces music, maintains a popstar structure, and attempts to guarantee profits, those in the margins typically include independent record companies and artists who provide creativity for new styles, which are then sometimes absorbed into the nucleus and marketed to a broad audience. A prime example of this process can be seen in the mainstream success of "grunge," an alternative rock style from the city of Seattle, which was rapidly appropriated by the major record companies in the early 1990s.

American influenced popular music is seen by some as an encroaching force upon the cultural identities of foreign nations, while others see it as a wonderful gift to the world. Historically, Canadian talent has made important contributions to American popular music. Nonetheless, Canada has been striving to protect and develop its musical culture from this irrefutable American influence since the introduction in 1971 of legislation to create minimum levels of Canadian content in domestic media. This landmark policy is believed to have engendered a self-sustaining Canadian music industry via the development of domestically produced popular music. The juggernaut that is American musical creativity and influence cannot be underestimated and its evolution is revealed in the pages you are about to turn.

I sincerely hope that this book will allow you, the reader, to better understand how and why popular music has evolved into one of the twenty-first century's undeniable cultural and social forces.

Enjoy the read,
Mark Vinet

Calixa Lavalleé

Thomas Edison

Al Jolson

Cole Porter

1st row: Richard Rodgers & Oscar Hammerstein
2nd row: George Gershwin & Ira Gershwin
3rd row: Irving Berlin

Bing Crosby

Frank Sinatra

1.   ORIGINS, TRADITIONS & HISTORY

Modern popular music in North America originated in Old World Europe. Historically, European popular music consisted of songs of the medieval troubadours and minstrels mixed with elements of fine art or classical music originally intended for a small, elite audience but that became widely popular. After the British Industrial Revolution, the popular music of the eighteenth century Victorian era and the early 1900s was that of vaudeville and the music hall. Its upper reaches were dominated by waltz music and the operettas of composers such as Gilbert & Sullivan, Victor Herbert, Tchaikovsky, Jacques Offenbach, and others. In North America, meanwhile, popular music evolved in its own unique way.

The most popular songs in North America during the late 1700s, according to sales of printed sheet music, were written by professional British composers for recital in London parks or for performance in British ballad and comic opera. The songs often had pastoral themes, were romantic in content, contained ethnic stereotypes, and included Scottish and Irish words and melodies. By the early 1800s, Italian opera had also become popular in North America. Songs by Italian composers were published as sheet music. In addition, the Italian "bel canto" or soft style of singing was to have an influence on the development of the clear, light, intimate, and sentimental style of singing known as "crooning" that became popular in Canada and the United States during the 1920s & 30s.

Prior to the American Revolutionary War (1775-1783), virtually the only music published in the North American Colonies was religious music. Most of it consisted of settings of hymns and psalms by various composers including William Billings. Billings operated singing schools with the goal of building a market for this type of music. People also sang these pieces in church, at family gatherings in homes, and in singing societies.

British abolitionist and Reverend John Newton, a reformed merchant slave trader, collaborated with poet William Cowper on several editions of *Olney Hymns*, which achieved lasting popularity. The first edition, published in 1779, contained two hundred and eighty pieces by Newton including the world-famous hymn that celebrates his amazing transformation, *Amazing Grace.*

Composed between 1760 and 1770 in Olney, *Amazing Grace* was possibly one of the hymns written for a weekly service. Although the hymn was not originally entitled *Amazing Grace*, it later came to be known under that name. Through the years, other writers have composed additional verses to the hymn and possibly, verses from other Newton hymns have been added. The origin of the melody is unknown. Most hymnals attribute it to an early American folk melody, while others speculate that it may have originated as the tune of a song that slaves sang.

Nonreligious music also flourished in the British and French colonies, but much of it was passed orally from person to person, without being published. British colonists sang secular folk and popular songs from England and songs written by North Americans in the English style. Many songs were sold on large sheets of paper with words printed on one side called "broadsides". The broadsides provided no music, only lyrics, with instructions that they were to be sung to a well-known melody.

Throughout the colonial period (1607-1776) black slaves often performed as musicians at social functions. They played instruments from Africa, including forerunners of the banjo. They also played the violin and other European instruments.

Extensive publication of secular music began in North America in the 1790s. During the post-Revolutionary War decades (1784-1840), most North American music publishing companies were located in the populated northeastern cities of Boston, Philadelphia, Baltimore, New York City and Montreal. These companies published collections of songs and instruction books for such instruments as violin, flute and fife. In addition, sheet music, usually for solo voice with piano accompaniment, began to appear. Most of these volumes contained military marches, dances, and other recognizable songs of the time. Also common and popular were booklets called "songsters". Like broadsides, most songsters included only the lyrics to be sung to well-known tunes.

Throughout this period, North American popular music continued to be greatly influenced by music from overseas. Great Britain's Henry Bishop, for example, composed/arranged the music to *Home, Sweet Home*, probably the most popular tune of the nineteenth century. American poet John Howard Payne wrote the lyric. Between 1808 and 1834, Irishman and poet Thomas Moore wrote new words for traditional

Irish Melodies. Among the popular titles in Moore's collection, known in North America, were *Believe Me If All Those Endearing Young Charms* and *'Tis the Last Rose of Summer*.

During the pre-American Civil War years (1841-1861), North American popular music began to develop its own identity. Minstrel theater shows became a dominant form of popular stage entertainment. In minstrel shows, troupes of white performers disguised as blacks – by wearing blackface makeup – performed songs, dance routines, and comedy skits, that reflected their conceptions of African American life and music. Mid-1800 minstrel shows acted out crude parodies of African American behavior. They were performed in a spirit of parody and did not present authentic black music. Although, these "black face" entertainers impersonated blacks, they did introduce some basic elements of African American music to large white audiences for the first time. The instruments minstrels played were characteristic of slave music. Minstrel entertainers played fiddles, tambourines, bones, and incorporated the technique of banjo playing used by African American musicians. The minstrel stage had a strong impact on the development of popular music. American performer Thomas Dartmouth "Daddy" Rice demonstrated the profitability of minstrel music with his 1829 song *Jim Crow*, which was the first American song to become a worldwide sensation. Many minstrel songs were successful in sheet music form, and they became an important force in the development of nineteenth century popular song. Ohio composer Daniel Decatur Emmett's popular songs *Old Dan Tucker* of 1843 and *Dixie* of 1859 were first performed on the American minstrel stage. *Dixie* made its Southern debut in New Orleans and quickly became the favorite of all Confederate songs during the Civil War. The tune also accompanied Jefferson Davis's inauguration at Montgomery, Alabama, on February 16, 1861. *Dixie* was the most parodied of all the Southern songs during the War. Even Northerners wrote some *Dixie* parodies but despite its Northern origins, Dixie belonged to the South.

The first important composer of North American popular song, and the most influential American songwriter of the mid-nineteenth century was Pittsburgh native Stephen Collins Foster, who rose to fame writing more than two hundred songs for minstrel shows. The best-known troupe of the 1850s was Christy's Minstrels, which popularized many of his songs. Foster was at the forefront when white American culture started to integrate black culture to its own. His melodies are so much a part of American history and culture that most people think they're folk tunes. Foster was the first North American to make his living as a songwriter, making him the first true "king of pop". Many of his best-known original songs, such as 1848's *Oh! Susanna*, 1850's *Camptown Races*, 1851's *Swanee River* aka *Old Folks at Home*, 1854's *Jeanie with the Light Brown Hair*, and one of his most lyrical compositions *Beautiful Dreamer* published the year of his death in 1864, are perennial favorites. Foster was a genius at creating simple, compelling combinations of words and melody that would become known in popular music as a "hook", meaning a catchy musical phrase that hooks the listener's ear. Though he virtually invented pop music as we now recognize it, Foster's personal life was tragic and contradiction-riddled. His marriage was largely unhappy, he never made much money from his work and he died at the young age of 37 a nearly penniless alcoholic on the Bowery in New York City.

The Hutchinson Family – a singing group made up of three brothers and a sister from New Hampshire – also gained notoriety in the 1840s. They were among the first North American performers to use popular music as a vehicle for social commentary. For example, some of their songs promoted temperance and protested slavery. During the Civil War they helped popularize the pro-Union song *Lincoln And Liberty*. Also during this period, emancipated American slave William Wells Brown published a compilation of anti-slavery songs, hoping to build sympathy for the anti-slavery agenda. This along with his other literary publications, helped establish his reputation as the most prolific black American man of letters of the mid-1800s.

The African population, shipped to the Americas in chains as slaves, originated from many different West African regions, tribes, and villages; each with their own language and musical culture. In order to thwart any plans of revolt, they were separated, thereby denied a common means of verbal communication. These immigrant captives turned to the music they new for comfort. This mixing of music most likely led to the unique rhythms that eventually formed the bedrock of North America's modern popular music. When slave-owners outlawed African drums, slaves compensated by incorporating percussive elements into their playing of other instruments and their singing styles.

Later, African American slaves used music and lyrics to orally express their suffering. Many of these songs are now recognized as the forerunners of more modern Black American musical forms including spirituals, the blues, and ultimately, jazz. The intent of this slave music and the human suffering that lay behind it conveyed a strong message to those who listened. Joshua McCarter Simpson, from Ohio, was one such African American poet whose memorable songs of emancipation were set to popular tunes and sung by runaway slaves traveling the Northern Underground Railroad. Canadian bound runaways often sang inspirational songs. A version of the song "The Free Slave" by the American abolitionist George W. Clark illustrates this well. Crossing the border Suspension Bridge into Canada at the Niagara frontier, fugitive slaves sang songs, which in many ways captured the spirit of their personal heroic journey, while at the same time rendering homage to the many great escape stories that marked the Black experience in North America.

The American Civil War (1861-1865) was of great importance to North American popular music. Citizens often expressed in song the strong feelings aroused by the conflict. As a result, there was a tremendous increase in composition and publishing. Such songs as *The Battle Cry of Freedom* and Julia Ward Howe's celebrated *Battle Hymn of the Republic* of 1862 expressed Northern Unionist sentiments. Southern Secessionists, meanwhile, expressed the attitudes of the Confederacy in 1861's *The Bonnie Blue Flag*. The former song was second only to *Dixie* in popularity among confederate soldiers. English born vaudeville performer Harry Macarthy wrote *The Bonnie Blue Flag*, setting it to a well-known Irish tune. When Union General Benjamin F. Butler was commander in New Orleans, he banned the song, fined anyone who sang it, fined the publisher, and confiscated the plates from the printer.

During the war singing was one of the soldiers' favorite pass-time. Numerous tunes were written and sung throughout the armies and at home. On the field, fifers played shrill tunes accompanied by drummers beating various beats. The songs sung during the conflict can be divided up into several distinct categories. There were inspirational marching tunes written to boost the morale of soldiers on both sides; Negro spirituals and other traditional slave songs; sad sentimental tunes that soldiers sang when they were melancholy and lonesome for home; there were songs that home-front families sang when thinking of loved ones away at war; songs of the Union and of the Confederacy; of Abraham Lincoln; dialect, minstrelsy, and humorous songs; and those inspired by the battles and campaigns.

Civilians, for the most part, sang the sentimental songs. Soldiers preferred the rousing marching songs, satiric songs, protest songs and parodies that sprang spontaneously from army life. Both sides enjoyed singing Stephen Foster's songs.

Music was a basic element in everyday life for the soldiers. For example, during the battle of Gettysburg, the Confederate regimental band played waltzes and polkas. Sometimes, if soldiers liked a tune they heard the enemy singing, they would write their own lyrics to the song and sing it themselves. For this reason, many Civil War songs have at least two versions.

In the Confederacy, poems about the war were published in Southern periodicals. Those that captured the ears of tunesmith were set to music, and published as songs. Northerners also composed and published poems about the war and some of these too, were later published as songs. But the majority of the Northern tunes were written as songs to begin with, and published as sheet music or in small paperback books. The song sheets were often sold for ten cents per copy, and thousands were distributed free to the soldiers.

In November, 1861, Harper's Weekly published a poem by Ethel Beers called *The Picket Guard*, which, when put to music by Baltimore's John Hill Hewitt, became known as *All Quite Along The Potomac Tonight*. Both Confederates and Unionists sang parodies of popular songs such as *Wait For The Wagon*. The lyrics were simply changed to suite the allegiance of the target audience. James Randall, another native of Baltimore, was in Louisiana when he heard the news of fighting in his native city in April 1861. He immediately wrote the poem *Maryland, My Maryland*, and the New Orleans Delta newspaper published it on April 26. Miss Jennie Cary, also of Baltimore, set the poem to the tune of a popular college song. The piano arrangement on the original sheet music came from Charles Ellerbrock, who composed the music for *God Save The South*. *The Yellow Rose of Texas* was a popular minstrel love song. The term "yellow" in the tune refers to a light-skinned black American or mulatto. Southern supporter F.W. Rosier wrote words to the French national anthem for the *Virginian Marseillaise*. During the war, the *Marseillaise* was so strongly identified with the Confederacy that a French theatrical troupe was arrested in Manhattan for singing the anthem during their performance. Union Troops marched to a number of songs from the American Revolution, including *Yankee Doodle* and *Hail Columbia*.

Songs were written about traitors and dissenters on both sides. *Abraham's Daughter*, aka *The Raw Recruit*, was a favorite in the North. Soldiers wrote parodies on it, and minstrel troupes sang it everywhere. Septimus Winner, who wrote the tune, was a Northern Democrat. Later in the war he wrote a song in defense of General George B. McClellan, whom Lincoln had just relieved as commander of the Union armies. Winner was accused of treason for writing that song.

In army camps and on the battlefield, instruments were critical as a means of communication. Drumbeats served to tell soldiers what to do, and to keep them in step. Drum calls issued commands to soldiers, while other drumbeats with fife accompaniments helped soldiers march. Fife music was popular during the war because the shrill tone of the fife could be heard well above the rumbling of cannon and the other noises on the battlefield. Buglers were indispensable in the war because they too were responsible for sounding out commands. These included reveille in the morning, numerous calls throughout the day, and tattoo at night, as well as field commands such as advance and retreat.

The Civil War also had an impact on popular music in many other ways. It provided musical training for soldiers who played in military bands. In addition, the so-called War Between the States brought people from different parts of North America together. These contacts enabled people to learn about one another's musical traditions, styles, instruments, and songs. Of particular importance was the exposure many whites gained to authentic black music, notably the religious songs called "spirituals". The all black Fisk Jubilee Choir led by George White first popularized the spirituals. Up to this time, most Northern whites' conception of black music had come only from blackface minstrelsy.

Of the fifty thousand Canadian-born soldiers who fought for the North and South in the bloody four-year conflict, a French Canadian soldier named Calixa Lavallée would return to Canada after the war and work as a professional musician and composer. He would one day compose the music for Canada's national anthem "O Canada".

Emancipation in the United States after the war allowed a greater number of former black slaves to become professional songwriters and musicians. Black groups who specialized in singing spirituals became popular in the late nineteenth century. During the 1870s, a distinct genre of popular American hymnody emerged. At first a style predominantly popularized by whites, it became prominent in the urban religious revivals led by the evangelist Dwight Moody with the musician Ira Sankey.

Its roots were in camp meeting spirituals, Sunday school hymns, and the harmonies and melodies of popular music. The lyrics often dealt with conversion and salvation.

With the winds of change, brought about by the Civil War, the Southern United States became fertile ground for new musical idioms during the late nineteenth century. Instruments rarely used by black slaves, such as guitars, pianos, and horn instruments, became central to the new genres of black American music that developed and flourished. In addition, all-black minstrel troupes were formed during this era. A new style called the "blues" became popular in the early 1900s. The blues most likely developed from work songs and the calls known as "field hollers" that plantation laborers used as a form of communication in the fields.

Ragtime, a style of music often played on the piano, emerged in the 1890s in the American Midwest – principally in the city of St. Louis, Missouri. It quickly became the most popular music style in North America. Ragtime was an energetic variety of music that emphasized formal composition. It combined many elements, including syncopated rhythms and the harmonic contrasts and formal patterns of European military marches. Ragtime traced its' roots to plantation melodies and dance music such as the "cakewalk", to minstrelsy, and to music for black stage shows. Early in ragtime's development, professional composer Scott Joplin began writing formal compositions in the ragtime style. Ragtime soon acquired mass popularity throughout Europe and flourished worldwide in the first two decades of the twentieth century; giving birth in the 1920s to the Charleston dance craze.

Another new style of music called jazz developed in the cosmopolitan city of New Orleans, Louisiana around the year 1900. During the late 1800s African Americans combined complex African polyrhythms with European harmonic structures to create what would become the most important new musical style of the twentieth century. Jazz also represented another important stage in the influence of black music on mainstream popular music.

Jazz was partially rooted in African American dance music, as well as in the brass band music played in New Orleans during parades and funeral processions. Noisy taverns became the usual setting for dancing. The piano replaced the banjo and fiddle as the favorite means of providing dance music. During the nineteenth century, a new type of musical variety show called "vaudeville" replaced the minstrel show as the foremost live-entertainment medium. Like minstrel shows, vaudeville consisted of songs, comedy routines, dances and other skits. The two differed, however, in that vaudeville reflected Northern white influences rather than black Southern culture. Vaudeville was at the peak of its popularity from the 1880 to 1939.

By the late nineteenth century, the music-publishing business was centralized in an area of lower Manhattan Island in New York City, to be known as Tin Pan Alley. The genre took its name from the byname of the street on which the industry was based, around 28th Street between Fifth Avenue and Broadway Street in the early twentieth century; around Broadway and 32nd Street in the 1920s; and ultimately on Broadway between 42nd and 50th streets. The area got its name from the noise of the cheap loud pianos furiously pounded by the so-called "song pluggers" demonstrating tunes in music publishers' offices. Musicians sometimes referred to these pianos as "tin pans".

During the late 1800's, traveling tent shows, medicine shows, Wild West shows, and printed sheet music brought pop music from Northern industrialized cities into the rural South. The first pop song to sell one million sheet music copies was the 1892 tune *After the Ball* by songster Charles K. Harris. Its success sparked growth in the music-publishing industry. Composers were hired to rapidly produce pop songs by the dozens, and the techniques of Stephen Foster and other Tin Pan Alley composers were further developed and refined. Tunes had to be simple, catchy, and emotionally appealing to sell to broad audiences. Singers such as Sophie Tucker and Al Jolson promoted Tin Pan Alley songs on North American vaudeville tours.

Tin Pan Alley emerged as the world's first self-contained popular song-publishing industry, and in the ensuing fifty years, its prolific lyricism was combined with European operetta in a new type of musical play known as the musical comedy, or "musical". A musical is a kind of stage-play that tells a story through a combination of spoken dialogue, tunes, and dances. New York City was the thriving and vibrant center of musical comedy, the successor to vaudeville. Many of the tunes published by Tin Pan Alley originated in musicals. Tin Pan Alley controlled the publication of popular music throughout the early twentieth century, and musicals remained an important means for introducing new songs to the listening public. Musical comedy achieved great sophistication in the hands of composers who wrote many popular songs during this vibrant epoch.

The golden age of Tin Pan Alley occurred during the 1920s and

30s. The best-known songs of this epoch were produced by a small group of lyricists and composers based in Manhattan. These talented songwriters included Cole Porter, Irving Berlin, Aaron Copland, Jerome Kern, and pianist Thomas "Fats" Waller who wrote the song *Ain't Misbehavin'*. In many cases, composers and lyricists worked in teams of two such as brothers George and Ira Gershwin, Richard Rodgers and Lorenz Hart, and beginning in 1943, Richard Rodgers and Oscar Hammerstein II. Tin Pan Alley songs were popularized in Broadway musicals and by popular singers accompanied by dance orchestras. Important technological innovations, including the rapid spread of commercial radio, also occurred during this era. The development of more affordable and better-quality shellac phonograph discs made recordings more popular than sheet music, and the introduction of amplified electric recording led to the development of crooning, the intimate and sentimental vocal style perfected by talented singers such as Bing Crosby and, later, Frank Sinatra. Sinatra opened a new window onto pop music by changing 32-bar music with personalized phrasing and an induplicable storytelling vocal style. Few singers delivered a lyric like Sinatra.

New York's Tin Pan Alley comprised the commercial music of songwriters of ballads, dance music, vaudeville, and musicals, and its name eventually became synonymous with North American popular music in general. When these styles first became prominent, the most profitable commercial product of the many music publishing companies lining Tin Pan Alley was sheet music for home utilization. Songwriters, lyricists, and popular performers labored to produce music to meet the demand. The growth of film, audio recording, radio, and television created an increased need for more and different types of music, and Tin Pan Alley's dominance diminished drastically as other music-publishing centers arose to supply songs for these different genres.

The audience for popular music quickly grew in the first half of the twentieth century, partly because of wider technological innovations and developments. Sound recording, invented and patented in 1877 by the American Thomas Edison, became an important way to distribute popular music in the early twentieth century. Gramophone discs soon surpassed printed sheet music as the primary means through which popular music was disseminated. By the mid-20s, almost 110 million records were produced and sold each year in North America. Songwriters and publishers were no longer the main force in popular music. Instead, music began to be dominated by artists and record companies. The rise of sound recording also altered the ways in which people enjoyed pop music. Instead of gathering around the piano in homes to sing the latest tunes themselves, people played recordings of other people singing. By 1930, phonograph records had replaced sheet music as the main source of music in the home, thereby enabling persons without any musical training to hear popular tunes. At the same time, the use of the microphone relieved vocal performers of the need for professionally trained voices that could fill large concert spaces, thereby allowing intimate vocal techniques to be commercially adapted. Record companies discovered and exploited new markets during the early twentieth century. In the process, they helped popularize several styles of music that eventually evolved into twenty-first century popular music.

Pop music idioms clearly tended to move westward from Europe to North America until the early twentieth century, when American ragtime and Broadway musicals found receptive audiences in Europe. Since then, Western popular music has been dominated by developments in North America. North American pop music achieved unquestioned international prominence and dominance in the decades after WW II.

Joan Baez

Bob Dylan

2. FOLK

Folk music consists of a people's unique traditional songs and melodies. It is known, accepted and embraced by a significant number of people in a society and may be thought of as expressing the character of a nation, country or of a social, occupational, ethnic, or regional group. Folk songs deal with almost every kind of human activity and are considered the music of the people. Many of these songs express the spiritual or political beliefs of a nation or an ethnic group, or explain their history. For example, North American traditional indigenous "pow wow" music properly meets these criteria.

Folk music, also called "roots music", is generally understood by broad segments of the population, while classical or cultivated music is mainly the art of a small economic, intellectual, and social elite. Folk music typically was circulated within families and restricted social groups. It is closely related to pop music in several ways. Societies possessing popular music also have a folk music tradition.

Generally, folk music is learned by listening to another person rather than by reading the musical notes or words. It thus consists of songs or pieces taught through performance rather than written musical notes or "notation". In essence, it is music learned by memory and passed on to others. Unlike traditional folk music, popular music is written by known individuals, usually professionals, and does not evolve through the process of oral transmission. Folk music is passed from person to person, from generation to generation, and from place to place. A folk song does not have a standardized form. The melody and words of a song may develop over a long period of time. Its words as well as its music exist in more than one and sometimes a great many variants, or in slightly different versions. Over the years, a tune may change a great deal, either from a desire for change or by accident. A song may be lengthened or shortened, or its rhythms and pitches modified. Part of one song may be combined with part of another. In these ways, families of songs are created. The words of a tune also may evolve over time. In addition, one set of words may be sung with different melodies, or different words may be sung to a single melody.

Folk music usually is written and performed by nonprofessional musicians. In many cases, the original composers of a song or melody are anonymous or forgotten. Traditionally, folk performers have been amateurs within rural communities rather than professionally trained urban musicians. However, songs by professional composers are considered folk music if they become part of a people's traditional music.

Each folk culture has a large number of instruments, with several basic instruments in common. These instruments include simple flutes, rattles, Jew's harps, wooden trumpets, drums and other percussion. Historically, these instruments have also been used by children as toys or by adults as part of community rituals. Some instruments traveled from one culture to another. Many instruments were originally developed in urban cultures including the accordion, clarinet, and double bass. These instruments were adopted for folk music without much alteration. Other instruments originated in classical or fine art music but later were used primarily by folk musicians. Examples include mandolins, guitars, the hurdy-gurdy and dulcimers. Traditional North American instruments used to accompany folk songs include the fiddle, banjo, guitar, and harmonica.

Many folk music instruments are played solo, but ensembles or groups are also common. Folk ensembles generally resemble chamber music ensembles rather than orchestras in that no two instruments play precisely the same part. Many other ensembles combine one melody-producing instrument with drums and other percussion. Although many folk artists are accomplished musicians, folk music is simpler and more compressed in style than classical or serious art music.

Folk music exists in many different forms and under a variety of cultural, economic, and social conditions. Folk music is found in most of the world's societies. Historically, folk music is most commonly the music of the socially and economically lower classes and of rural populations living in villages, hamlets or small towns. Different than the music of tribal societies, folk music is often viewed as the music of people without a higher education in societies that have a more educated class. This politically and economically elite stratum of society maintains the so-called classical music culture.

There are many types of folk songs, including folk theater songs, tunes that address important occasions, children's songs, marching songs, and religious songs. Folk music is closely associated with everyday activities such as spirituality, work, and family life. Some folk tunes have no words, only a melody. Instrumental folk music of this type goes with marching and dancing, which is occasionally accompanied by singing.

The ballad or narrative epic is one of the main types of western European and North American folk songs. A ballad tells a story, usually based on true events. Ballads have a stanza form, in which a melody is repeated for each of several verses. There may also be a chorus or refrain that is sung several times during the tune. Some ballads describe legendary events that happened long ago while others are based on more recent actual incidents. Many ballads tell about the deeds and exploits of heroes or villains, as well as famous or infamous characters. For example, the American Civil War tune *John Brown's Body* honors a well-known abolitionist, viewed by his contemporaries as either a hero or a villain. The stories of the origin of the song are numerous and varied. One story has it originating spontaneously from a parade in Boston shortly after Brown was hanged. The song was often referred to as the "emancipation Marseillaise," and enjoyed popularity among black and white Union soldiers.

Many folk songs reflect outstanding events in a nation's history. For example, Canada's 1759 Battle of the Plains of Abraham inspired the earliest known Anglo-Canadian ballad, *Brave Wolfe* or *Bold Wolfe*. The War of 1812 produced such lively tunes as *Come All You Bold Canadians* and *The Chesapeake and the Shannon*. Other ballads recall the Rebellions of 1837-38 and the Fenian raids of 1866, and Confederation in 1867 inspired some anti-Confederation songs in Newfoundland. Newfoundland is particularly rich in the ancient supernatural ballads that are rare elsewhere in North America.

Some folk songs deal with a particular set of circumstances, including love, prison life, natural disasters, and war. For example, the Civil War Confederate song *The Battle Of Shiloh Hill* effectively described the realities of war with the killing, suffering and dying. The song remains in oral tradition in the Southern Appalachian Mountains. Other folk songs deal with a specific activity, occupation or job. For example, people sing some work tunes as rhythmic accompaniment to repetitive labor. Songs with texts that concern farming activities and other kinds of labor can build the solidarity and morale of the working group. Work songs were created to help long days pass more quickly or to sing after work. Historically, laborers as diverse as cowboys, farmers, miners, longshoremen, and sailors sang popular work songs. Some union songs called for improved working conditions.

Harvard graduate John Lomax was best known for collecting and preserving American folk songs for the Library of Congress folk song recording program. Lomax and his son Alan toured prisons in

Louisiana and Texas, asking for and listening to songs. He wanted to find the songs that real people sang in their everyday life. He called himself a "ballad hunter". Lomax thought prisons would be a good place to find songs, because inmates didn't have a chance to hear much music except the music they made themselves. Some of the most famous songs he heard, recorded on portable equipment set up in the truck of his car, and wrote down were *Home on the Range* and *Swing Low, Sweet Chariot*. The most famous prisoner Lomax interviewed was Huddie Ledbetter, also known as Leadbelly, at the Louisiana State Penitentiary in Angola, in 1933. Lomax helped Leadbelly get paroled. When he got out of prison, Lomax took him on a concert tour and recorded many of his songs. At first, Leadbelly would appear on stage wearing prison strips. Lomax spent the rest of his life collecting and preserving American folk songs. From 1933 to 1941 he collected over twelve hundred discs containing over four thousand songs.

Although the folk music of European cultures is very diverse, they share some important attributes and characteristics. The music is relatively simple, usually consisting of tunes with a repetitious form. Most folk songs themselves, while spreading as variants, remain in their homelands. Occasionally, however, they pass from one nation to another, their style altering in the process.

North American folk music is known for its high level of energy, intensity, humor, and emotional effect. The key influences on North American folk music came from England, France, other European countries, and from the continent of Africa. Various ethnic groups preserve the folk music of their ancestors by holding festivals during which traditional music is performed. In addition, the songs of North American aboriginals have made an important contribution to the heritage of North American folk music. Contemporary Robert Mirabal combines traditional Native American music with popular forms to create a new type of cutting edge pop music.

The North American colonists from the British Isles and France brought their folk music traditions with them, especially ballads and instrumental dance melodies. Later immigrants from other nations also brought their own folk music, which combined and interacted with the British and French music in multiple ways. The African slaves who were shipped to the Americas had different musical traditions from those of Europeans. For security reasons, many slave masters did not allow the Africans to speak their tribal language or perform their indigenous music on the plantations. As a result, the exact words and melodies of the songs were eventually forgotten. The black slaves, however, retained the essence and style of their music and created new songs that combined African and European traditions. Many of these songs followed the "call-and-response" pattern, in which a leader sings a line and the entire group answers. Percussion instruments were played to create a loud and complex rhythmic accompaniment.

Black slaves sang about their suffering in spirituals, such as *Go Down, Moses*. Prior to the Civil War, escaped slave Harriet Tubman helped 300 people escape slavery. Her code name was "Moses," and she is said to be the Moses referred to in this traditional black spiritual. In the 1960s, black Americans sang *We Shall Overcome* and *Free at Last* to emphasize their struggle for civil rights.

Some folk songs simply provide amusement and are meant only to entertain. Dance songs, game songs, and comical songs, are only intended to make people enjoy themselves in the company of family and community friends. There are also religious folk songs, children's songs, and songs that mark the changing seasons or the important stages of a person's life.

Folk and popular music tended to merge in the twentieth century. Much of what is presently called folk music in English-speaking territories is a subcategory within popular music. It is the product of urban professionals who appropriated authentic folk music idioms for stage and recorded performances. Most folk cultures changed dramatically during the twentieth century, especially after WWII. Falling cultural, political, and geographical barriers led to a wide dissemination of folk music via the introduction of printed sheet music, then radio and phonograph records, later through films and television, and finally the Internet and other electronic forms of communication. Many small communities have acquired access to the same cultural materials and styles once available only in big cities. The musical ideals and lifestyle of rural people are now almost identical with those of urban people. The notions of regional isolation, distinctiveness, and ethnicity once associated with folk music have changed, as almost everyone has easy access to the sounds of folk music from many countries.

While this availability makes the typical musical experience of each person potentially more varied, it also forces a kind of conformity and uniformity on the world's musical culture. The modification of many folk instruments to make them compatible with modern stage and concert formats and electronic equipment also reduces cultural distinctions. The combination of musical idioms from various parts of the world with European-based harmonies, instruments, and song structures in the world music movements has greatly changed the concept of folk music. These recent developments had antecedents in the early part of the twentieth century. Members of American folk communities from rural Appalachia, for example, moved to urban centers and continued their traditions in modified form. European ethnic groups now living in North American cities preserve their ethnic integrity and musical traditions at festivals and social gatherings.

A series of folk music revivals beginning in the Great Depression of the 1930s brought the performance of traditional and new folk songs to the middle classes of North American and Western European cities, as well as to college campuses. Dissenting political and social movements made use of folk music as a rallying cry at various times in the twentieth century. The radical European Fascist right of the 1920s and 30s, the North American liberal movements of the 1930s and 40s, the American civil rights movement of the 1960s, and the international movement against the Vietnam War (1954-1975) in the late 60s and early 70s produced agitation and protest songs that used popular folk melodies and imitated the styles of folk songs.

Several modern styles of popular music mix folk and pop elements. For example, there has been some interaction between folk music and rock music, as the designation "folk rock" indicates. Folk rock arose in North America in the 1960s. In its texts, it is modern urban folk song, with topical issues, often on current social and moral subject matter. Musically, however, it has the characteristics of rock in its electrified string band and rhythmic percussion accompaniment.

In the late 1950s, traditional white American folk music experienced a revival and gained new popularity. Merle Travis wrote about the hardships of coal mining in his hit song *Sixteen Tons*. His innovative acoustic guitar playing, known as "Travis picking", made it possible for solo musicians to play rhythm and melody simultaneously. The New Lost City Ramblers presented folk music while playing traditional instruments. Young, urban, college-educated artists such as the Kingston Trio had several hits with traditional folk ballades. Woody Guthrie, a native of Oklahoma, inspired many artists in this folk music resurgence. Guthrie composed over one thousand songs that used traditional folk influences, styles and melodies, including *This Land Is Your Land* in 1965. Many folk singer-composers with a social conscience began writing their own songs and a number gained immense popularity. The best known of these songs were frequently concerned with protests against war or social problems such as the Depression dust bowls, poverty, gender discrimination, the plight of Native Americans, and racial prejudice. The leading social protest singer-songwriters included Joan Baez and Pete Seeger who first found success with his group the Weavers.

Artists, such as American singer Judy Collins, also used folk music to bring awareness to environmental conservation efforts. Bob Dylan, whose songs include *Blowin' in the Wind* of 1962, *The Times They Are A-Changin'* of 1963, and *Like a Rolling Stone* of 1965, was the most important writer and best-known of the folk singers produced by this movement. Several of Dylan's compositions were later re-recorded or "covered" with greater commercial success by pop artists including Joan Baez, Peter, Paul & Mary, and the Byrds.

International liberation movements in Quebec, Northern Ireland, among the Basques of northern Spain, and among various ethnic groups from Central and Eastern Europe have also produced major folk song artists. Quebec's Gilles Vigneault and the 1980s Irish group called the Chieftains are examples of nationalist folk musicians.

The use of folk music for political purposes was prominent in Eastern Europe and the former Soviet Union. Not long following WWII, governments in these areas founded schools to train folk musicians who would then work as concert performers representing both Russian nationalism and Communist populism. After 1950, Eastern European countries raised money to support their folk traditions through festivals, community gatherings, and competitions.

Modern tourism has also had an important impact on folk music culture. For example, in almost all parts of Europe the conservation of folk traditions is encouraged, while at the same time causing them to be changed to meet entertainment expectations and tastes of international tourists.

Although folk music includes a great variety, modern popular music has mainly been influenced by folk music of the nineteenth and early twentieth centuries in North America and Western Europe. Folk music has continued to alter in style, method of transmission, and social context. The differences separating folk music from other types of music, however, have become less visible. Despite the apparent loss of distinctions in world musical folk culture, its mass appeal persists as a worldwide phenomenon and its influence on modern popular music continues unabated.

top left: Leadbelly, top right: Bill Broonzy
center: Robert Johnson
bottom left: Muddy Waters, bottom right: John Lee Hooker

B.B. King

Ray Charles

clockwise from top left: Stevie Ray Vaughan,
George Thorogood, Colin James, Bonnie Raitt

3. BLUES

The blues is a genre of secular African American folk and popular music. It is a musical style created in response to the hardships endured by generations of black American people. It originated in the rural Mississippi Delta region of America's Deep South at the beginning of the twentieth century. The monumental importance of blues on modern popular music is not to be underestimated.

Blues is primarily a vocal narrative style featuring solo voice with instrumental accompaniment in repeated 12-bar sequences. Blues lyrics tend to deal with the general hardships, challenges, and difficulties of life and the sorrows of love. They are typically presented in three phrases consisting of an initial phrase, its repetition, and a new third phrase. The sung words are normally followed by instrumental improvisation, creating a call-and-response pattern, whereby a vocalist or musician will sing or play a phrase and another singer or musician will respond with another phrase. African influences are apparent in the blues form including tonality, the call-and-response pattern of the repeated refrain structure of the blues stanza, the artificially high voice or "falsetto" break in the singing idiom, and the imitation of vocal styles by instruments, especially the harmonica and guitar.

Blues singing, rooted in various forms of black American slave song, developed in the South after the American Civil War. It was influenced by work songs and field hollers, minstrelsy, ragtime, spiritual, sanctified Baptist church music, and the folk and popular music of whites. By the 1920s, the blues style had acquired its distinguishing characteristics of harmonic structure, melodic shape and text. Although instrumental accompaniment is universal in the blues, the blues are essentially vocal. The singer expresses his emotions rather than tells a story, making blues songs lyrical rather than narrative. The feelings expressed are generally those of sadness, often due to vicissitudes in love. Even though the blues is performed in a melancholy manner, it is designed to make the listeners feel happy. To express this musically, blues artists use vocal techniques such as falsetto and syncopation and instrumental techniques such as bending guitar strings on the neck or "choking", or applying a metal slide or knife to the guitar strings.

Melody is shaped by strongly influenced "blues notes" that sound like "bent" or flattened 3rd , 5th , and 7th notes of the major scale.

Blues notes have a bittersweet emotional impact. Although vocals are the focus, performers usually improvise instrumental solos. In addition, performers can also contribute improvised "fills" at the end of a sung line in a kind of call-and-response style. One musical innovation was the development of the "bottleneck slide" style of guitar playing by heavy delta blues and gospel performer Eddie James "Son" House Jr, who developed the technique on his National steel-bodied guitar. The bottleneck method consists of scraping a glass bottleneck up the guitar fingerboard to create a whining, voice-like sound, thereby simulating vocal moans and slides. Son House's heavy, raw slide guitar playing and intense vocals marked him as one of the most powerful blues performers ever heard.

Blues derived from and was largely played by southern African American men, most of whom were farm laborers. The earliest references to blues date back to the last decade of the nineteenth century. The rural blues developed in three main regions, the states of Mississippi, Georgia and the Carolinas, and Texas. Mississippi Delta blues is the most intense and influential of the three styles. Vocally it is the most speech-like, and the guitar often makes use of a bottleneck or slide accompaniment and is percussive and rhythmic. The Mississippi style was well represented by performers such as Son House, Mississippi John Hurt, the Jelly Roll Kings trio, Charley Patton, Willie Brown, Skip James, Johnny Shines and Robert Johnson.

American blues composer, guitarist, and singer Robert Johnson influenced both his contemporaries and many later musicians with a haunting falsetto singing voice and masterful, rhythmic slide guitar. He played an emotional and inventive style of Delta blues. Born into the large family of a sharecropper, Johnson grew up in Memphis, Tennessee and the Mississippi Delta region. He learned to play the harmonica and then the guitar, probably influenced both by recordings and by personal contact with well-known Mississippi Delta bluesmen. He traveled widely throughout the southern states of Tennessee, Mississippi, Arkansas and Texas, and as far north as the cities of Chicago and New York, performing at juke joints, lumber camps, house parties, and on the street. In 1936-37 he made a series of recordings in San Antonio and Dallas, Texas. His repertoire included several compelling original tunes such as *Me and the Devil Blues, Love in Vain*, and *Hellhound on My Trail*. Despite the limited number of his recordings, Johnson had a great impact on other musicians and recording artists. Johnson died of poisoning in 1938 at the age of 27 after drinking strychnine-laced whisky in a juke joint.

Best known as a traveling companion of Robert Johnson, Johnny Shines' own contributions to the blues have often been under-appreciated, simply because Johnson's own legend casts such a long shadow. Shines was one of the top slide guitarists in Delta blues, with his distinctive, energized style. Shines eventually made his way to Chicago, and made the transition to electrified urban blues, helped in part by his robust, impassioned vocals.

The blues of Georgia and the Carolinas are celebrated for their regularity of rhythm and clarity of enunciation. Influenced by white roots music and ragtime, they are more melodic than the Mississippi and Texas styles. Blind Boy Fuller and Blind Willie McTell were representative of this style.

The Texas blues are noted by high, clear vocals accompanied by supple guitar lines that consist of single-string picked arpeggios rather than strummed chords. The most prominent Texas bluesman was, without a doubt, Blind Lemon Jefferson who greatly influenced 1950s Mississippian electric bluesman J.B. Lenoir. Texas also produced seminal gospel-blues artist Blind Willie Johnson, regarded as one of the greatest bottleneck slide guitarists. His 1927 recording of *Dark Was The Night* was included on the disc of sounds attached to the 1977 Voyager deep space spacecraft. Over the years, many artists have covered the gospel songs made famous by Johnson.

The earliest blues, known as "archaic", "country" and "delta" blues, were a product of the nineteenth century Southern rural experience, especially after emancipation. These blues styles differed widely in their musical and lyric structure and form. Vocalists usually accompanied themselves on harmonica or guitar. Itinerant performers, generally men, traveled from one town to another singing about freedom, love, sex, the hardships of life, and even the devil himself.

At the dawn of the twentieth century, blues gradually became more of an urban phenomenon as rural black Americans migrated to big city urban areas such as New Orleans, Memphis, and Nashville, looking for work. "Classic", "city" or "urban" blues evolved in the 1920s and 30s and featured a male or female stage vocalist usually accompanied by a piano or backed by a whole jazz band. Musical and lyric structures and forms became largely standardized. Adapted to solo piano, city blues gave rise to "boogie-woogie" piano playing.

Black women made the first blues recordings in the 1920s. These performers were primarily stage singers backed by jazz combos.

New York vaudeville singer Mamie Smith's 1920 recording of *Crazy Blues* launched the "race recording" industry, which targeted blues and jazz directly at the African American market. These recordings proved popular with a wider American audience as well, and blues recordings by singers such as Bessie Smith, Ida Cox, Gertrude "Ma" Rainey, and seminal jazzmen Jelly Roll Morton and Louis Armstrong dominated the musical arena. Throughout North America blues could be heard in barrooms, rent parties, small dance halls, and juke joints, where virtuoso pianists such as Clarence "PineTop" Smith performed new styles such as "barrelhouse" and boogie-woogie.

Capitalizing on the increasing popularity of urban blues, the music industry began publishing and marketing arrangements for blues compositions. In 1912, with the publication of *Memphis Blues* by black bandleader and composer William Christopher "W.C." Handy, blues entered the realm of popular song. Another important composition by Handy was *St. Louis Blues* of 1914. Blues songs became so fashionable and successful that many popular Tin Pan Alley songs that were not actually blues simply added the word "Blues" to the title to ensure their popularity.

W.C. Handy was a key figure in the development of the blues. He took his themes from the blues musicians he heard daily, wrote them down, and harmonized them. Some blues was published prior to Handy, but, as a result of the distribution of his work, jazz players by the late 1920s were freely improvising and spontaneously inventing melodies on his blues chord sequences.

The world wars and the Great Depression caused the geographic spreading of the blues. The blues expanded and dispersed as millions of African Americans, along with many blues musicians, left the abject poverty, repressive Jim Crow segregation laws, and the Dixie cotton fields and tobacco farms for northern cities like Detroit, where the Ford Motor Company offered high paying jobs. During the Great Migration, black singers from the South moved north to industrial cities and a more sophisticated urban environment, to look for work. The older rural blues evolved into the rougher urban blues style, marked by freer vocal phrasing and larger bands. Lyrics took up urban themes, and the blues combos developed as the solo bluesman was joined by a pianist or harmonica player and then by a rhythm section consisting of bass and drums. The electric guitar and the amplified harmonica created a dynamic sound of driving rhythmic and harsh emotional intensity. The electric organ also came into use about this time. Among the cities in which the blues initially took hold were Detroit, Memphis, St. Louis and Atlanta. It was Chicago, however, that played the greatest role in the development of urban blues.

In the 1920s and 30s Memphis Minnie, Tampa Red, Big Bill Broonzy, brilliant harmonica player John Lee "Sonny Boy" Williamson and guitarist Robert Lockwood, Jr were popular Chicago performers in the noisy clubs of the city's Southside. After WWII they were supplanted by a new generation of bluesmen that included the beloved Chester Arthur Burnett aka Howlin' Wolf, Elmore James, Little Walter Jacobs, Otis Spann, and Mississippian Muddy Waters. Waters, considered the "godfather of the blues", pioneered the hard-edged electric Chicago blues by adding a driving drum beat and electric bass. Harmonica wizard James Cotton and gifted musician-composer Willie Dixon both joined Muddy's multi-talented combo.

Blues and jazz overlapped, sometimes almost indistinguishably, and blues was considered a nurturing form for early jazz, but blues also developed independently. In the 40s vocalists such as Aaron Thibeaux "T-Bone" Walker and Louis Jordan performed with big bands or with ensembles based on electric guitar, acoustic stand-up bass, drums, electric organ and saxophones. After 1950 two vanguard guitarists, Buddy Guy and Riley "B.B." King, intensified the sound of blues by amplifying the guitars and adding more emphasis to the drums. They used improved electric guitars that allowed for the manipulation of sustained tones, amplified electric basses, and brass instruments, which often replaced saxophones. B.B. King was musically nurtured on Memphis' Beale Street, a cultural center for blacks throughout the South and a rendezvous for different musical styles. In 1970, B.B. King released his signature song *The Thrill Is Gone*, earning him the accolade "King of Blues". Unlike traditional blues, the recording industry applied the terms "electric blues", "rhythm and blues" and, later, "soul" to blues and non-blues music performed in these electrically amplified blues styles. Soul music and rhythm and blues, aka R&B, show obvious blues tonalities and forms.

The birth of black radio in the 1950s made stars of the Memphis bluesmen, and they hit the road. The black clubs they played became known as the "Chitlin Circuit." The creator of a singular sound which he dubbed "folk-funk," multi-instrumentalist Bobby Rush was among the most colorful characters on the contemporary Chitlin Circuit, honing a unique style which brought together a cracked lyrical bent with elements of blues, soul, and funk.

The blues have influenced many other musical styles. It has contributed significantly to the development of jazz, rock music, and country music. Blues and jazz are closely related. Jelly Roll Morton and Louis Armstrong both employed blues elements in their jazz music. The blues, however, have had their greatest influence on rock music. Early rock singers often used blues material. During the 1950s white musicians adapted the electric blues style. White artists such as Bill Haley, Jerry Lee Lewis, and Elvis Presley, transforming R&B into rock and roll, often covered R&B hits. British rock musicians in the 1960s, especially the Rolling Stones, the Animals, Led Zeppelin, John Mayall, and Eric Clapton, were greatly influenced by the blues. These artists, along with such American rock musicians as Paul Butterfield, Mike Bloomfield, and the Allman Brothers Band, returned to the blues roots as the source for their heavily amplified hard rock style.

From its obscure origins among Southern blacks in the early 1900s, the blues' simple but expressive structures and forms had become in the mid-1960s one of the most important influences on the development of popular music. A 60s blues revival took place beginning at the 1964 Newport Folk Festival. Old bluesmen were invited to perform and thereby rediscovered and finally appreciated.

Although much of the energy of blues has been channeled into rock and R&B styles, traditional blues musicians such as Junior Wells, Etta Baker, and the "King of Boogie" John Lee Hooker, have enjoyed successful careers. Veteran bluesman Othar Turner was the last master of the Mississippi backcountry fife-and-drum tradition.

Blues has also developed into a major force in contemporary music through the rock-edged style of Stevie Ray Vaughan, George Thorogood, Bonnie Raitt, Robert Cray, and Canadian Colin James, as well as roots-oriented jazz by instrumentalists associated with Wynton Marsalis, the Zydeco sound, and some rap groups. Keb' Mo' draws on the old-fashioned country blues style of Robert Johnson, but keeps his sound contemporary with touches of soul and folksy storytelling. He writes much of his own material and has applied his acoustic, electric, and slide guitar skills to jazz and rock-oriented bands as well.

Perhaps the most fascinating and extraordinary thing about the blues has been its longevity and durability. Blues has retained its attraction for soloists of all eras and styles, changing with new approaches and movements but remaining intrinsically true to its roots.

top: Benny Goodman & his Orchestra
bottom: Glenn Miller & his Orchestra

Billie Holiday

Duke Ellington

Ella Fitzgerald

Nat 'King' Cole

Charlie Parker

John Coltrane

Miles Davis

Wynton Marsalis

4. JAZZ

Jazz is a popular and influential type of popular music that evolved from black folk songs and plantation dance music in the Southern United States. Jazz has borrowed from black folk music, and popular music has borrowed from jazz, but these three kinds of music remain distinct and should not be confused with one another.

Developed by African Americans at the dawn of the twentieth century, Jazz music gradually developed into a sophisticated modern art. Jazz is the audible history of racial integration in America and is considered the foundation of modern popular music, and the only true art form to originate in the United States. Jazz was actually widely appreciated as an important art form in Europe before it gained such recognition in North America. During WWI, black American James Reese Europe conducted the 369th Regiment "Hell Fighters" Band in France and gave many Europeans their first taste of ragtime and jazz.

Unique features of jazz are its sounds, rhythms and the ability to create new music spontaneously. As a basically improvised kind of music, jazz's mission has always been to express and transmit strongly felt emotions. Improvisation is the key element that gives jazz a fresh excitement at each performance. Improvisation transforms the soloist from a performer into a composer. This skill is the distinguishing characteristic of the true jazz musician.

Typically, the improvisation is accompanied by the repeated chord progression of a popular tune or an original composition. Although exceptions occur in some idioms, most jazz is based on the principle that an infinite number of melodies can fit the chord progressions of any tune. The instrumentalist improvises new melodies that fit the chord progression, which is repeated over and over again as each soloist is featured, for as many choruses as desired.

Although songs with many different formal patterns are used for jazz improvisation, two formal patterns in particular are often found in pieces used for jazz. One is the form of popular-song choruses and the second is the 12-bar blues form with roots deep in African American folk music.

Jazz music grew from a combination or "gumbo" of influences, including black American music, African rhythms, American band traditions and instruments, and European harmonies and forms. Jazz, however, is rooted in the musical heritage of American blacks, which includes traits surviving from West African music. West Africa may be economically poor but the culture is rich. Among the surviving African traditions are singing styles that include freedom of vocal color and improvisation, call-and-response patterns, and conflicting rhythms played by different members of a band and syncopation of individual melodic lines. Syncopation is an important element of jazz. To syncopate their music, jazz instrumentalists take patterns that are even and regular and break them up, make them uneven, and put accents in unexpected places.

Early Jazz also incorporated black folk music forms developed in the Americas such as rowing chants, lullabies, field hollers, and later, spirituals, gospel and blues. The blues is a form of music that has always been an important part of jazz. Its mournful scale and simple repeated harmonies helped shape the unique character of jazz. Jazz musicians have long exploited the blues as a vehicle for improvisation.

Jazz also borrowed from European popular classical music of the 1800s and 1900s, which contributed specific styles and forms including hymns, waltzes, mazurkas, military marches, quadrilles, and other dance music, light theatrical music, French and Italian operatic music, and also theoretical elements, in particular, harmony.

African American-influenced elements of pop music that contributed to jazz include the banjo music of minstrelsy, and the syncopated rhythmic patterns of black-influenced Latin American music played in southern American cities. Other influential elements include the barrelhouse piano styles of black tavern musicians in the Midwest, and hymns and marches, as they were played by African American brass bands in the late nineteenth century. Near the end of the 1800s, ragtime emerged and influenced early jazz as well.

After 1910 bluesman W. C. Handy took another influential form, the blues, beyond it's previously strictly oral tradition by publishing his original blues songs. Favored by jazz musicians, blues songstress Bessie Smith recorded many of them in the 1920s.

African Americans who had almost no training in Western music first performed early jazz. These musicians drew on a strong musical culture from black American life. As jazz grew in popularity, instrumentalists with formal training and classical backgrounds influenced its sound. During its prolific history, jazz has absorbed influences from the folk and classical music of Asia, Africa, and other areas of the world. The development of instruments with new and different features and qualities has also influenced the sound of jazz.

Most early jazz was played by solo pianists or in small marching bands. The repertoire included military marches, ragtime, hymns, spirituals, and blues. Although blues and ragtime had arisen independently of jazz, and continued to exist in parallel, these idioms influenced the style and forms of jazz and provided important conduits for jazz improvisation.

Jazz bands performed at weddings, birthdays, parades, picnics, and funerals. Typically, the bands played mournful dirges on the way to funerals and spirited up-tempo marches on the way back, modified often by acceleration and syncopations.

Almost every Western musical instrument and many non-Western instruments have been used when performing jazz. For example, the violin and vibraphone, an instrument similar to the xylophone, have been especially popular in combos. Jazz, may be played by one musician, by a small ensemble of pieces called a combo, or by a big band of ten or more musicians. A combo is divided into two sections consisting of a solo front line of melody instruments and a back line of accompanying instruments called a rhythm section. The front line consists of one to five brass and reed instruments. The rhythm section consists of piano, bass, acoustic or electric guitar, and drums. The front-line instruments play most of the solos. These instruments may also perform together as ensembles. A big band consists of brass, reed, and rhythm sections.

The rhythm section in a combo or big band maintains the steady beat and embellishes the rhythm with syncopated patterns. It also provides the formal structure to support solo improvisations. The drums keep the beat steady and add colorful rhythm patterns and syncopations. The piano or guitar plays the chords or harmonies of the composition in a rhythmic manner. The bass outlines the harmonies by sounding the roots, or bottom pitches, of the chords, on the strong beats of each measure. Any of the rhythm instruments, especially the piano, may also solo during a piece.

The principal brass instruments of jazz are the cornet, the slide trombone, and the trumpet. Secondary brass instruments are the valve trombone, the baritone horn, the flugelhorn, the French horn, and even electronic trumpets have been played in jazz performances.

The trumpet and cornet are melody instruments of identical range. But the trumpet is usually considered more brassy and the cornet mellower. The slide trombone blends well with the trumpet. The brass section of a big band typically consists of three trombones and four trumpets. Jazz trombonists and trumpeters often use accessories called mutes to change or modify the sound of their instrument. The musician plugs the mute into the bell or flared end of the instrument or holds it close to the opening of the bell.

The saxophone and clarinet are the principal reed instruments of jazz. The flute, though technically a woodwind, is frequently classified as a reed in jazz. It is used especially as a solo instrument. In early jazz, the soprano clarinet was an equal member of the front line with the cornet or trumpet and the trombone. The clarinet eventually gave way to the saxophone, which is capable of much greater volume. A reed section in a big band is typically made up of two alto saxophones, two tenors, and a baritone. Instrumentalists often play two or more reed instruments, such as an alto saxophone and a tenor saxophone, during a performance.

Drums of various types were familiar to African Americans dating back to the days of slavery. These early percussion instruments played a fundamental role in the development of jazz. As jazz grew, the drum kit evolved until one drummer could play more than one percussion instrument at the same time. The invention of a foot-operated bass-drum pedal and pedal-operated cymbals freed the drummer's hands to play other percussion instruments, such as snare drums, tom-toms, wood blocks, and cowbells. Another important invention was a wire brush that the drummer used instead of a mallet or drumstick to produce a more delicate sound on cymbals and drums.

The piano has historically been played both as a solo instrument and as an ensemble instrument that performs as part of the rhythm section. At present, other keyboard instruments, including electric pianos, electronic organs, and synthesizers, may substitute for pianos. The guitar, like the piano, is capable of playing both melodies and chords. In the early days of jazz, these two instruments, along with the banjo, were often substituted for one another. Later, however, the banjo and guitar were most often used in the rhythm section in addition to the piano. The banjo eventually disappeared from almost all later forms of jazz. Since jazz's beginnings, musicians have used the acoustic guitar in bands and as a solo instrument. In the late 1930s the electric guitar surfaced in jazz to add greater volume, sustained tones, and a new variety of effects and sounds.

The string bass or brass bass, such as a Sousaphone or tuba, plays the roots of the harmonies and co-anchors the rhythm section. When an electronic organ is used, the organist can play the bass part with foot pedals on the instrument. Electric bass guitars have also been incorporated into some jazz bands.

New Orleans Jazz is considered the earliest known fully developed jazz style to emerge. Centered in the southern city of New Orleans it was first heard at the beginning of the 1900s. The style developed from New Orleans's musical traditions of band music for black street parades and funeral processions. At present, this type of jazz is sometimes called traditional jazz, classic jazz, or Dixieland jazz. Volume and enthusiasm were more important than skill and finesse, and improvisation was focused on the group sound. In this style the trumpet or cornet carried the melody, the clarinet played countermelodies, and the trombone played rhythmic slides and sounded simple harmony or the root notes of chords. Below this basic trio the string bass or tuba provided a bass line and drums the rhythmic accompaniment.

New Orleans was the musical home of the first notable players and composers of jazz, including a black musician named Buddy Bolden who, prior to the age of recording, led some of the first jazz ensembles. By 1906, Bolden's cornet had become the most celebrated sound in Storyville, New Orleans's red light musical district.

Although some jazz influences can be heard on a few early phonograph records, not until 1917 did a jazz band record. This band, a group of five white New Orleans musicians calling themselves The Original Dixieland Jass Band, created a sensation in Europe and in North America. The record sold over 250,000 copies at seventy-five cents each and easily outsold top recording artists Enrico Caruso and John Philip Sousa. The band soon changed the spelling of "Jass" to "Jazz", played in Chicago, traveled to New York, and then to Europe.

The term "Dixieland jazz" eventually came to mean the New Orleans style as played by white musicians including the New Orleans Rhythm Kings. The most important series of recordings in the New Orleans style were done in 1923 by the influential stylist and cornetist King Oliver and the Creole Jazz Band. Other leading New Orleans artists included Mamie Smith who recorded *Crazy Blues* in 1920, the trumpeters Bunk Johnson and Freddie Keppard, the soprano saxophonist and clarinetist Sidney Bechet, the drummer Warren "Baby" Dodds, and the Creole pianist and composer Jelly Roll Morton. The most prominent musician nurtured in the "Big Easy", however, was King Oliver's second trumpeter and cornetist, Louis Armstrong.

The first true virtuoso soloist of jazz, Louis Armstrong was a true genius of feeling and the embodiment of jazz. To many he is America's Wolfgang Amadeus Mozart, Ludwig van Beethoven or Johann Sebastian Bach. His contribution to jazz and pop music is impossible to notate. Armstrong put the swing in jazz and created the vocabulary for swing. He was a dazzling improviser, technically, intellectually, and emotionally. He transformed the format and structure of jazz by bringing the soloist to the forefront, and in his recording combos – the Hot Five, Hot Seven, and Savoy Ballroom Five – demonstrated that jazz improvisation could go beyond simply enhancing the melody. Armstrong created new melodies based on the chords of the initial tune. He also became the first famous male jazz singer and, in a very real way, invented modern pop singing. He set standards for all later jazz vocalists, not only by the way he modified the lyrics and melodies of songs but also by popularizing "scat singing". By singing wordless syllables in an instrumental manner he mastered the ability to vocally improvise without words, like an instrument. Louis Armstrong made many of his most celebrated recordings, including *Heebie Geebies*, with his combos from 1925-28. These recordings rank among the masterpieces of jazz, along with his duo recordings of the same era with pianist Earl "Fatha" Hines including a King Oliver tune *West End Blues*.

The 1920s have been called the golden age of jazz or the "Jazz Age". For jazz the roaring 20s was a decade of significant discovery and experimentation. Recordings of blues, ragtime, and jazz of different kinds soon popularized the music to a greater audience. Commercial radio stations, which first appeared during that decade, featured live performances by the growing number of jazz musicians. As a result, Jazz then spread from New Orleans to other parts of the continent. The American cities of St. Louis, Kansas City, Memphis, and Detroit, were all fledgling jazz focal points.

The black American influence on mainstream pop music became stronger during the Jazz Age. As jazz spread across the continent, so did black musicians. Fate Marable led a New Orleans band that performed on riverboats traveling the Mississippi River. Jelly Roll Morton played throughout the United States and Canada. Many New Orleans musicians, including King Oliver and Louis Armstrong, migrated north to Illinois, influencing local Chicago musicians and stimulating the evolution of a type of improvisation and arrangement that became known as "Chicago style" jazz. A group of Midwest young men, many from Chicago's Austin High School, developed this new style. These white instrumentalists, known as the Austin High Gang, included pianist Joe Sullivan; clarinetists Frank Teschemacher, Pee Wee Russell and Mezz Mezzrow; trumpeters Muggsy Spanier and Jimmy McPartland; saxophonists Frankie Trumbauer and Bud Freeman; drummers Dave Tough and George Wettling; and cornetist Leon Bix Beiderbecke, whose lyrical, crisp and clear approach to the cornet provided an alternative to Louis Armstrong's trumpet style.

This new exciting and vibrant sound emanating from the "Windy City" derived from the New Orleans style but emphasized soloists, often adding saxophone to the instrumentation, and producing edgier rhythms and more complex textures. Musicians working in Chicago or influenced by the Chicago style included the trombonist Jack Teagarden, the banjoist and guitarist Eddie Condon, the drummer Gene Krupa, and the clarinetist Benny Goodman. They played harmonically inventive music, and the technical ability of some of the players, especially Goodman, was at a higher level than that of many past performers.

Many Chicago musicians eventually settled in New York City's Harlem district, another major mecca for jazz in the 1920s. Harlem was in the midst of a black cultural renaissance and jazz musicians joined right in, especially at the Savoy Ballroom. They loved the vitality of New York and gave the city its famous nickname, The Big Apple. There, piano music provided a fresh vehicle for jazz innovations. Harlem became the center of a highly technical and dazzling, hard-driving solo style known as "stride piano". In stride piano, the left hand plays alternating single notes and chords that move up and down the scale while the right hand plays solo melodies, interesting chordal passages, and accompanying rhythms. The master of this approach in the early 20s was James P. Johnson, composer of the *Charleston*. Fats Waller, Johnson's protégé, quickly became the most celebrated performer in this style. Johnson strongly influenced other jazz pianists, notably Edward Kennedy "Duke" Ellington, William James "Count" Basie, Mary Lou Williams, Teddy Wilson, who was featured with Benny Goodman's band in the 1930s, and Art Tatum, who performed mostly as a soloist and was regarded with awe for his multifaceted virtuosity.

Boogie-woogie was another jazz form that developed in the 1920s and became very popular during the 1930s and 40s. A style of blues chiefly played on the piano, it used eight beats to the bar instead of four and consisted of a short, sharply accented bass pattern played again and again by the left hand while the right hand played freely, using an assortment of rhythms. Boogie-woogie featured the traditional blues pattern for most themes. The music had a driving quality that created excitement through the repetition of a single phrase. Important boogie-woogie musicians included Albert Ammons, Pinetop Smith, Meade Lux Lewis, and Pete Johnson.

The most innovative keyboardist of the 1920s was Earl Hines, a virtuoso considered to possess a wild, unpredictable imagination. Earl Hines has been called the first modern jazz pianist. His playing differed from other pianists of the 20s in his use of what were then considered unusual rhythms and accents. His style, combined with the smoother approach of Fats Waller and comparable to Louis Armstrong, influenced most contemporary and later pianists.

Also during the 1920s, large ensembles of jazz musicians began to perform together. These so-called "big bands" were modeled after the society dance orchestras of that time period. These bands became so popular that the period was known as the big band or "swing era". The swing era flourished from the late 1930s to the mid-40s and got North Americans, especially teenagers, dancing wild new styles like the Jitterbug. Jazz enjoyed its only period of mass popularity during this period with the swing style of the big bands and with such crooner vocalists as Bing Crosby, Frank Sinatra, and later, Johnny Mathis, Dean Martin, Sammy Davis Jr, Vic Damone, Jerry Vale, Al Martino, Perry Como, Andy Williams, Frankie Laine, Wayne Newton, and Tony Bennett.

The emergence of the swing era injected a rhythmic alteration to jazz that smoothed the two-beat rhythms of the New Orleans style into a more flowing four beats to the bar. Instrumentalists also developed the use of pithy melodic patterns, called "riffs", in call-and-response patterns. To facilitate this process, bands were divided into instrumental sections, each with its own riffs, and opportunities were provided for instrumentalists to play extended solos.

During the 1920s, Duke Ellington led an orchestra at New York's famous Cotton Club in Harlem and at various downtown Times

Square nightclubs like the Roseland. It was at the Cotton Club that his sound, filled with trumpet growls, unusual harmonies, and chords no-one had ever heard before, was given a new name, and for some a demeaning name "Jungle music". The music was hot, exotic, and sexy. Ellington was a prolific composer who wrote colorful experimental concert pieces ranging in length from the three-minute *Koko* in 1940 to the sixty-minute *Black, Brown, and Beige* in 1943, as well as tunes such as *Solitude*, *Harlem Flat Blues*, and *Sophisticated Lady*. Continuing to conduct his band until his death in 1974, Ellington's music made his band a cohesive unit, with solos written for the unique features of specific instruments and performers. One of Ellington's protégés was the talented pianist Billy "Sweet Pea" Strayhorn, composer of the familiar jazz composition, *Take the A Train*.

In 1932, Duke Ellington recorded his famous composition *It Don't Mean a Thing If It Ain't Got That Swing*, an anthem for a new era. "Swing", which emphasizes four beats to the bar, was soon adopted as the name of the newest style of jazz. Big bands dominated the swing epoch, especially bands in the tradition of Ellington led by Chick Webb, Jimmie Lunceford, Cab Calloway, Count Basie, and Benny Goodman who became known as the "King of Swing".

Beginning in 1934, Benny Goodman's orchestras, bands and combos brought swing to North American audiences through concert halls, ballroom dance events, radio broadcasts, and recordings. Goodman was the first white bandleader to feature white and black musicians performing together in public. In 1936, he introduced two outstanding black soloists, vibraphonist Lionel Hampton and pianist Teddy Wilson. Until then, racial segregation had hampered the progress of jazz and of black artists in particular. In 1938, Goodman and his orchestra, and several virtuoso musicians, performed a prestigious concert at Carnegie Hall in New York City. Their famous performance was one of the first by jazz musicians in a concert hall.

Other leading orchestras of the swing era included those directed by brothers Jimmy and Tommy Dorsey, Woody Herman, Benny Carter, Andy Kirk, Bob Crosby, Earl Hines, Jimmie Lunceford, Artie Shaw, Stan Kenton, Chick Webb, Harry James, Gene Krupa, and American composer and trombonist Glenn Miller. Miller's triumphs in the ballrooms as a big band leader were based on sweet orchestrations meticulously executed. The Miller saxophone sound, instantly recognizable and much copied, was based on quite simple musical principles, as were all his big hits, including his own composition, *Moonlight Serenade*, which grew out of an exercise he had written while studying with Joseph Schillinger. Some aficionados contend that the jazz content of his orchestra was negligible, but others regard its sound as the definitive pop music of its era.

A different type of big band jazz was developed in the mecca of the mid-west Kansas City, Missouri during the mid-1930s and was epitomized by Count Basie's orchestra and its electrifying sound. Basie's band had a distinctive swing style that depended less heavily on written arrangements, allowing more room for extended solo improvisations and intense rhythms. Basie instead relied on the 12-bar blues form and riff backgrounds, which consisted of repeated simple melodies. Originally formed in Kansas City, Basie's "barons of rhythm" orchestra reflected the southwestern emphasis on improvisation, keeping the written or memorized passages relatively short and simple. The wind instruments in his orchestra exchanged riffs in a free, strongly rhythmical interplay, with pauses to allow for extended instrumental solos. Basie's tenor saxophonist Lester Young, in particular, played with a rhythmic freedom rarely seen in the improvisations of soloists from other orchestras. Young's flowing melodies and delicate tone, sprinkled with an occasional trend setting gurgle or honk, opened up a new approach, as Louis Armstrong's trumpet playing had done in the 20s.

The foremost type of pop music from the mid-1930s to the mid-40s was big band swing, a style modeled on the innovations of black jazz orchestras. Jazz became a dominant influence on North American pop music during this period. In 1935, Benny Goodman ignited the popularity of the style with his orchestra's recordings of arrangements by Fletcher Henderson, a black New York City bandleader whose success had been limited by racial segregation. The development of the big band as a jazz vehicle was largely the achievement of Henderson, who is widely considered the first major figure in big band jazz. He became the first leader to organize a jazz band into sections of brass, reed, and rhythm instruments. In 1923, Henderson and his arranger, Don Redman, were the first to introduce and master the technique of scoring music for big bands, but they also attempted to capture the quality of improvisation that characterized the music of smaller ensembles. Various Henderson bands of the 20s and 30s included such jazz solo instrumentalists as saxophonists Benny Carter, the gifted tenor saxophonist Coleman Hawkins, and the brilliant Louis Armstrong.

Jazz singers came into prominence during the swing era, many performing with big bands. These refined vocalists included Jimmy Rushing, Ethel Waters, Mildred Bailey, Joe Turner, Ella Fitzgerald, Dinah Washington, Billie Holiday, Carmen McRae, Ivie Anderson, Lena Horne, Peggy Lee, Sarah Vaughan, Jack Teagarden, and Nat "King" Cole. In addition to singing, Jack Teagarden was a superb jazz trombonist and Nat King Cole was an excellent jazz pianist. His daughter, Natalie Cole, also became a fine vocalist.

During the late 1920s and early 30s, jazz advanced from relatively simple music played by musicians who often could not read music to a more sophisticated and complex form. Among the instrumentalists who brought about this change were Benny Carter and fellow saxophonists Coleman Hawkins and Johnny Hodges; the team of violinist Joe Venuti and guitarist Eddie Lang; and pianist Art Tatum. Many music connoisseurs consider Tatum the most inspired and technically gifted improviser in jazz history. Other avant-garde jazz artists of the 30s were the trumpeter Roy Eldridge, the drummer Kenny Clarke, the vibraphonist Lionel Hampton, the pianist-vocalist Hoagy Carmichael who co-wrote the ballad *Star Dust*, and the electric-guitarist Charlie Christian, who performed with Benny Goodman.

Since the days of ragtime, jazz composers had admired classical music. Attempting to fuse jazz with light classical music, celebrated white musician and band-conductor Paul Whiteman put some of the more obvious melodic and rhythmic aspects of jazz to good use in his orchestrations and recordings. Whiteman's orchestra also premiered jazzy symphonic pieces by American composers such as George Gershwin's *Rhapsody in Blue*. A number of swing-era instrumentalists "jazzed the classics" in recordings such as *Bach Goes to Town* by Benny Goodman and *Ebony Rhapsody* by Duke Ellington. Composers of classical concert music, in turn, paid tribute to and acknowledged the spirit of jazz in their works.

In the early 1940s, a group of young musicians began experimenting with more complicated melodic ideas and chord patterns in a combo setting called The Billy Eckstine Orchestra. The band included pianists Earl "Bud" Powell and Thelonious Monk, drummers Kenny Clarke and Max Roach, trumpeter Fats Navarro, and alto saxophonist Charlie "Bird" Parker. The group also included trumpeter Dizzy Gillespie, known for his formidable speed, fast runs, range, and daring harmonic sense. Recognized for his signature bent trumpet and legendary expanding cheeks when playing, it is a generally held belief that the modern trumpet style began with Gillespie's unbelievable concept of virtuosity. One of the pre-eminent jazz singers of the period, Sarah Vaughan, was also associated early in her career with these musicians, particularly Gillespie and Parker.

The style these two men developed became known as "bebop", rebop, or bop. In an era of fresh sounds, bebop was one of the freshest. Charlie Parker became the leader of a new bebop style. He was the most prominent and influential jazz musician of the 1940s. He created beautiful melodies that were related in advanced ways to the underlying chords, and his music possessed endless rhythmic diversity. Parker was a master of his craft and could do anything on the saxophone, in any tempo and in any key. Like Charlie Christian, Lester Young, and other virtuoso soloists, Parker had played with big bands but preferred smaller ensembles. Bebop's innovations were musically controversial and faced heavy resistance from critics and the musical establishment. In time, however, the style was better understood and came to be quite popular.

During WWII, the wartime economy and changes in public tastes had driven many big bands out of style, and business. The Big Band Era ended after the war when pop vocalists became more popular than bandleaders, although the influence of swing music could still be heard in "jump band" R&B and western swing music. The decline of big bands, combined with the radically new bebop style, led to a revolution in the jazz world.

Bebop was still based on the principle of improvisation over a chord progression, but the tempos were quicker, the phrases longer and more complicated, and the emotional range expanded to include more disturbing and unpleasant feelings than before. Jazz instrumentalists became aware of themselves as serious and mature artists and made little effort to sell their product by adding vocals, dancing, and comedy, as had their predecessors.

Most bop performers had an exceptional technique. They played long, dazzling phrases with many notes, difficult intervals, unexpected breaks, and unusual turns in melodic direction. On slower tunes, they displayed a sharp ear for subtle changes of harmony. Only extremely skilled instrumentalists were able to play bebop well, and only sophisticated audiences initially appreciated it. In bebop concerts, instrumentalists usually played an elaborate melody, followed with long periods of solo improvisation, and revisited the theme at the end of the piece. The bassist presented the basic beat for the band by playing a steady, moving bass line. The drummer enriched the beat with sticks or brushes on cymbals, snare drum, and tom-tom. The bass drum was reserved for surprise accents called "bombs". The pianist inserted intricate chords at irregular intervals to suggest, rather than state, the complete harmonies of the piece.

Most musicians, particularly on the American East Coast, continued to expand on the hard driving bebop tradition. Bebop was followed in the 1950s by "hard bop", "funky jazz", and "East Coast style". These forms emphasized some of the traditional values of jazz derived from blues and gospel music, including rhythmic drive, uninhibited tone and volume, and freedom from restricting arrangements. Major exponents of the East Coast style included the trumpeter Clifford Brown, the drummers Max Roach and Art Blakey, and the tenor saxophonist Sonny Rollins, whose idiosyncratic approach made him one of the great talents of his generation. Art Blakey led a combo called the Jazz Messengers from the mid-1950s until his death in 1990. The Jazz Messengers served as a training ground for many of the best soloists in jazz history. Another derivative of the Charlie Parker bebop style was "soul jazz", played by the pianist Horace Silver, the alto saxophonist Cannonball Adderley, and his brother, the cornetist Nat Adderley.

The late 1940s introduced an explosion of experimentation in jazz. Bandleader Stan Kenton brought forth a modernized sound that flourished alongside small bands with innovative musicians such as the pianist Lennie Tristano. Most of these bands drew new ideas from contemporary classical pieces. The most influential of the mid-century experiments with classically influenced jazz recordings made by Charlie Parker's protégé, a young trumpeter named Miles Davis. The written arrangements, by Davis and others, were soft in tone but highly complicated. Many bands adopted this so-called "cool jazz" style, especially on the American West Coast, and so it also became known as "West Coast jazz".

Cool jazz originated in the works of such musicians as Lester Young and Charlie Christian. In the late 1930s and early 1940s, these men made alterations in the sound and style of jazz improvisation. For example, they softened the tones of their instruments, used syncopation more subtly and delicately, and played with a more even beat. In 1948, tenor saxophonist Stan Getz recorded a slow, romantic solo of Ralph Burns's composition *Early Autumn* with the Woody Herman band. This work profoundly influenced many younger musicians including Miles Davis, who would soon achieve popularity with his blend of classical music and jazz.

In 1949 and 1950, Davis recorded several new compositions with a group of young virtuoso players that included alto saxophonist Lee Konitz, tenor saxophonists Stan Getz and Zoot Sims, baritone saxophonist Gerry Mulligan, and arranger Gil Evans. These seminal recordings emphasized a lagging beat, soft instrumental sounds, and unusual, sometimes bizarre orchestrations that included the first successful use of the tuba and the French horn in modern jazz. The recordings, with Davis as leader, were later released with the title *The Birth of the Cool*.

Cool jazz flourished throughout the 1950s and many combos became identified with the cool movement. Some of the most successful were the Gerry Mulligan Quartet, the Modern Jazz Quartet, and the Dave Brubeck Quartet, led by refined pianist Brubeck himself, with the alto saxophonist Paul Desmond.

In the 1940s and 50s, the sophisticated forms of cool and bebop jazz began to gain wide acceptance among intellectuals and university students. Jazz concerts suddenly became popular and bands hit the road on regional "territory tours". The best-known jazz names made a series of worldwide tours called *Jazz at the Philharmonic*. The international growth of jazz resulted in many successful overseas performances by American groups.

The invention and subsequent commercial introduction in 1948 of the long-playing "LP" vinyl record, also helped spread the popularity of jazz. For decades, jazz recordings had been limited to 10 inch 78 rpm (rotations per minute) records that restricted performances to about 3 minutes in length. The 12-inch LP permitted recorded performances to run longer. The LP also allowed a number of shorter performances to be issued on a single 7 inch 45 rpm record.

The first overseas jazz musicians to influence North Americans were Belgian guitarist Django Reinhardt in the late 1930s, and George Shearing, a blind, British keyboardist who immigrated to North America in 1947. During the 1950s, jazz instrumentalists in other countries began to improve greatly as they were exposed to American performers through live concerts and recordings. Other countries developed musicians and composers whose work compared favorably with that of the leading North Americans.

In 1954, the first large American jazz festival was held in the east coast state of Rhode Island at Newport. Since then, annual international jazz festivals have featured almost all of the most popular jazz musicians and have introduced many extended concert works in major cities around the world, including New York City, Chicago, Montreal, Berlin, Nice, Warsaw, Monterey in California, Montreux in Switzerland, the French Quarter in New Orleans.

Beginning in the 1950s, jazz music became even more experimental. Jazz began to feature non-traditional instruments and musicians began to take an interest in non-Western music, arrangements of scales or modes, melodic forms, unusual meters such as 5/4 7/4 9/8, and instruments of Asia and Africa. Several new approaches characterized jazz during the Cold War era. The late 1950s and early 60s ranked with the late 1920s and the late 1940s as one of the most rich and innovative periods in the history of jazz. Aficionados experimented with the abstractness and emotional rawness of modern jazz.

During this experimental period, innovative pianist George Russell developed a jazz theory of modes. In the late 1950s, classical musician and composer Gunther Schuller, together with the pianist John Lewis, musical director of the Modern Jazz Quartet, fused jazz and classical music into a "third stream" by bringing together players from both genres in a repertoire that consciously drew on the techniques of both types of music. Pianist and conductor Stan Kenton, one of the most exciting and controversial figures in jazz, also played orchestral works that combined elements of modern jazz and classical concert music.

In 1955 Miles Davis organized a quintet that featured the highly original tenor saxophonist John Coltrane, whose passionate approach produced a striking contrast to Davis's rich-toned, unhurried, expressive melodic lines. Coltrane poured out streams of notes with velocity and fervor, exploring every melodic idea, no matter how eccentric. He played slow ballads with self-assurance and composure, and in his solos he exposed an amazing sense of form and pacing.

In 1959, the Davis' combo, with pianist Bill Evans and saxophonists Cannonball Adderley and Coltrane, recorded an album consisting of compositions and improvised solos based on modes rather than on patterns of chords. Together they devised a set of pieces that remain in one key, chord, and mode for as long as 16 measures at a time, leading to the term "modal jazz". This landmark album, entitled *Kind of Blue*, introduced a revolutionary sound that allowed much freedom for the improviser.

Striking out solo, John Coltrane first pushed the intricacy of bop to its limits in 1959's album *Giant Steps*, and then settled on the other extreme, modal jazz. The latter style dominated his repertoire after 1960, when he recorded *My Favorite Things* using an open-ended arrangement in which each soloist stayed in one mode for as long as he desired. Coltrane's quartet included the pianist McCoy Tyner and the drummer Elvin Jones, two instrumentalists who, because of their dramatic musical qualities, were widely revered and imitated. It was during this period that the influence of the music of India entered jazz through Coltrane's adaptations.

Most controversial was the work of the alto saxophonist Ornette Coleman, whose improvisations, at times almost atonal, did away with chord progressions altogether, while maintaining the steady rhythmic swing so distinctive of jazz. Although Coleman's wailing sound and raw technique alarmed many critics, others recognized the humor, honesty, and rare sense of form that characterized his solos. In 1960, Coleman recorded the groundbreaking album *Free Jazz* with a double quartet. In this recording, Coleman discarded harmony, melody, and regular rhythms. He substituted unstructured improvisation played in no definite key or atonally.

Coleman inspired a whole school of "avant-garde jazz" that flourished in the 1960s and 70s and included the Art Ensemble of Chicago, the clarinetist Jimmy Giuffre, pianist Cecil Taylor, and even Coltrane, who ventured into avant-garde improvisation and conducted similar atonal experiments before his death in 1967. Also productive during this period was the composer, bassist, and bandleader Charlie Mingus, who performed his atonal, chord-progression-based improvisations with an uninhibited, rough excitement.

Meanwhile, the mainstream of jazz, although incorporating many of Coltrane's melodic ideas and even some modal jazz pieces, continued to build improvisations largely on the chord progressions of pop songs. The trio formed by the Bill Evans treated pop songs with depth, the musicians constantly interacting instead of simply taking turns for solos. This interactive approach was brought even further by the rhythm section of Miles Davis's quintet of 1963, which included the bassist Ron Carter, the pianist Herbie Hancock, the drummer Tony Williams, and later the tenor saxophonist Wayne Shorter.

Latin American songs, especially those in the Brazilian samba and bossa nova styles, were popular in the early 1960s. Their wild and exciting Latin rhythms and fresh chord progressions appealed to many jazz musicians, notably Stan Getz and flutist Herbie Mann. As a result of this Latin music boom, many bands augmented their regular drum kit with Caribbean percussion.

During the late 1960s, jazz suffered a dry spell and suffered an economic crisis. Younger "baby boom" audiences favored soul music, R&B, and rock. In the hopes of regaining an audience, jazz moved away from its recent seriousness and instead drew ideas from pop music. Some of these pop-oriented ideas came from rock, while others were drawn from the dance rhythms and chord progressions of R&B and soul musicians. Some jazz bands also added elements of music from other cultures. In 1969 Miles Davis recorded *Bitches Brew,* a very successful album that combined soul rhythms and electronically amplified instruments with unrelenting, highly discordant jazz. This ferment of sounds and styles became known as "fusion jazz".

Fusion combined the improvisational and melodic aspects of jazz with the instruments and rhythms of popular music. Electronic music played a major part in fusion. Jazz keyboardists began exploring the increased sound potential of synthesizers. String and horn musicians began to use electronics to distort, multiply or intensify their sounds. Many celebrated jazz players gained new popularity by performing fusion. In addition to Miles Davis, some of the most popular fusion musicians were trumpeter Donald Byrd, keyboardist Herbie Hancock, guitarist George Benson, and two ensembles, the Mahavishnu Orchestra and Weather Report, co-lead by Wayne Shorter and the Austrian-born pianist Joe Zawinul.

Alumnus of Davis's bands, including British electric guitarist John McLaughlin and the dazzling pianist Chick Corea's group Return to Forever, created some of the most musically successful fusion recordings of the 1970s. Rock groups such as Chicago, Chase and Blood, Sweat and Tears also began featuring jazz phrasings and solos over a rock-based rhythm. Together, they blended rock with the improvisation techniques of jazz to create a new form called "jazz-rock".

At the same time, another Davis alumnus, the unconventional pianist Keith Jarrett, succeeded commercially while avoiding electronic instruments and pop styles. His performances of pop standards and original compositions with a quartet, as well as his improvisations alone at the piano, marked him as a major contemporary keyboardist of jazz. During this same period, many veteran jazz musicians retained their popularity by leading bands that played in the cool, bebop, and swing styles. These seasoned bandleaders included Dizzy Gillespie, Woody Herman, Stan Getz, Gerry Mulligan, and Canadian pianist Oscar Peterson.

American jazz musicians were present in Canada by the late 1910s, among them Jelly Roll Morton, based in Vancouver, British Columbia in 1919-20. Young Canadians began to play the new music almost without delay. The many styles of jazz, from traditional, through Dixieland, swing, mainstream and bebop to contemporary, fusion and the avant-garde have all had their adherents in Canada. Not until the 1940s, however, did individual figures such as Peterson and the multi-instrumentalist big band leader Bert Niosi gain national recognition through their tours and radio broadcasts. Many other talented musicians have led successful big bands and jazz orchestras in Canada, including Montreal's Vic Vogel and Oliver Jones. It was Oscar Peterson, however, who emerged as the most internationally celebrated Canadian musician in jazz along with the iconoclastic Montreal group Uzeb.

In the mid-1980s there was renewed interest in serious jazz on the international front. A number of young jazz musicians rediscovered the mainstream jazz elements of cool, bebop, and swing styles. Linked with this interest was the brilliant trumpeter Wynton Marsalis, who was also highly praised for his performances of classical music. Marsalis soon became the most widely acclaimed young musician of the 1980s, playing with dazzling technique, refinement, and tone. Wynton has led several superb hard bop combos, and has also shared the stage with his instrumentalist father, and three brothers, including acclaimed saxophonist Branford Marsalis.

Despite this apparent return to basics, many young players continued to forge ahead with fusion bands. Two of the most widely respected fusion musicians are the brothers Brecker, saxophonist Michael and trumpeter Randy. In addition, Jane Ira Bloom displays a virtuosity of the synthesizer and soprano saxophone, versatile guitarist Pat Metheny continues to stretch the boundaries of jazz with his music.

In the 1980s, some "New Wave" jazz artists adopted minimalism, a style that often repeats simple patterns for long periods of time. Trombonist George Lewis has experimented with combinations of "free jazz", African rhythms, synthesized sound, and unusual horn techniques. Another trombonist of magnificent technique is Ray Anderson. Bebop, pop, rock, free, and various blends are all mixed in his recordings.

One ensemble, the World Saxophone Quartet, boldly removed the rhythm section while keeping most of the other traditional harmonic, melodic, and rhythmic elements of jazz.

By the early 1990s, a new generation of young jazz musicians had emerged, impressed and inspired by the artistic and commercial success of Wynton Marsalis. Many of these artists have merited critical accolades including pianist Marcus Roberts; saxophonists Scott Hamilton, Donald Harrison, and Christopher Hollyday; trumpeters Terence Blanchard, Philip Harper, and Roy Hargrove; guitarist Howard Alden; and trombonist Dan Barrett.

Throughout the last decade of the twentieth century, jazz continued to feature a variety of styles. Electronics technology took a larger role in jazz with the contributions of such young jazz composers as Michael Daugherty, who demonstrated that live musicians could interact creatively with computer-generated sound. On the other hand, many musicians chose to play in historic styles such as bebop and swing, while others sought a more experimental angle. Ornette Coleman's band Prime Time, for example, mixed free and fusion jazz in new and exciting ways, while the Art Ensemble of Chicago blended free jazz, exotic instruments, African makeup and costumes, and surprise techniques into theatrical musical events.

The new millennium bodes well for jazz with numerous young artists recording and performing in all genres. One such musician is a sultry vocalist and pianist Norah Jones. Jones developed her unique blend of jazz and traditional vocal pop with hints of bluesy country and contemporary folk due in large part to her unique upbringing in New York City as the daughter of renowned musician Ravi Shankar. She was lured to the Greenwich Village folk coffeehouses and jazz clubs and soon became inspired to write her own songs. Jones signed to Blue Note Records and released her debut album in 2002, garnering much public attention and several Grammy awards. Her crossover jazz-pop style is reminiscent of the 1980s success of Harry Connick, Jr.

Although twenty-first century jazz remains essentially the provenance of American musicians, and much of the best jazz is still written and performed in the United States, its international audience has flourished to the extent that musicians from many other countries are making major contributions to jazz and have formed an increasingly significant subgroup within jazz.

top: Hank Williams Jr
bottom: Hank Williams Sr

Johnny Cash

Dolly Parton

Kenny Rogers

Alabama

Garth Brooks

Shania Twain

5. COUNTRY

Country Music is a style of twentieth century popular music that originated among whites in rural areas of the Southern and Western United States. Born out of the folk music of the Southern Appalachia Mountain region in eastern Kentucky and Tennessee, country music is a major component of modern popular music. It encompasses the dance and narrative styles known as old-time, Cajun, cowboy, bluegrass, honky-tonk, Western swing, rockabilly, the Nashville sound, and the pop-oriented new country.

Over the years, country music has been influenced by folk, gospel, soul, R&B, and rock music and in turn has had an impact on these popular idioms. Although originally known by the derogatory and derisive label "hillbilly music," country has since moved into the pop music mainstream and gained worldwide acceptance. The label "country-and-western" music was adopted by the recording industry in the late 1940s to replace the term hillbilly music. Today's popular usage is simply "country" music.

The roots of country music lie in the ballads, folk songs, and popular songs of the English, Scots, and Irish settlers of the Appalachians and other parts of the South. Different types of music combined to form the basic sound of early nineteenth century country music, including Anglo-American folk ballads and fiddle tunes from Britain, Irish reels and the blues of Southern blacks, southern spiritual music, and American popular songs from the 1800s.

Beginning in the seventeenth century, immigrants from the British Isles brought their folk music to what is now the Southern United States. The music featured singing and fiddling. Such music was performed from colonial times in both religious and social contexts. Solo fiddlers played dance music at weddings, barn dances, and church services. One person accompanied by a fiddle often sang ballads and folk songs. By the early twentieth century, mail order catalogs and traveling salesmen made banjos, guitars, and mandolins widely available to people in the rural South. These instruments combined with the fiddle to form the basic country string band.

British folk music blended with the church music of the rural South. This religious music included hymns, and beginning in the late nineteenth century, gospel tunes, and spirituals. In the 1920s and 30s, congregations sang "shaped-note" music by reading symbols in a hymn book, and Southern bands played stringed instruments and sang gospel songs as well as old love ballads and folk songs, collectively called "old time music".

Since blacks and whites lived together in the South, they shared their traditional styles of music. Lyrics, form, song structure, and rhythmic guitar styles absorbed from the blues music of black Americans are part of the folk heritage of country music. One of country music's first stars, Jimmie Rodgers, performed in a style influenced by African American blues singers. Rodgers composed blue yodels, which combined story tunes similar to English ballads with the mournful and melancholy performance style of the blues.

Country music is about tradition, yet its simple form lends itself to endless variations on similar themes. Like blues, the two genres often shared themes, melodies and songs. Country is a simple music at its core and can be identified by its instrumentation, song lyrics, and vocal style. It is one of the easiest musical styles to create and one of the least intimidating to listen to. These basic qualities contribute greatly to its popularity. This fundamental aspect of country music stems from the fact that it is traditionally based on lyric content rather than musical content. In country, the primary purpose of the musical elements of melody, harmony, and rhythm is to showcase the words without distracting from them. Exceptions to this general rule include the purely instrumental music from country's early days and the technical skill often found in the bluegrass style.

Country harmony generally relies on a simple selection of a few repeated chords. Vocals usually appear as single lines, occasionally harmonized with high, closely spaced voices, most often in the chorus of a song. Rhythmically, there is little syncopation. Melodies are characteristically just as basic as the rhythm. Many country songs sound very similar and are discernible by their words.

Country lyrics tell stories in clear, unpretentious, simple language. A country song's lyric theme is frequently repeated as a hook in the chorus section. Most traditional country lyrics employ relatively few words, evoking a compact poetic effect. The words of country songs often describe the common experiences of ordinary, working-class people and cover such subjects as love, romance, cheating, relationships, loneliness, poverty, religion, hardships, and work. Some are happy songs, while others explore the loneliness and sense of loss that result when love goes wrong or when married folks are unfaithful. Some country tunes have sacred themes, mirroring the traditional importance of religion in Southern life. Other country songs offer advice on a range of topics, including on how life should be lived. They express sorrow about the loss of a rural or agricultural way of life and the loss of closeness among families, friends, and neighbors. Some country songs describe historical events or everyday happenings in the news like wars, natural disasters, unemployment, and homelessness.

Country artists usually sing in a clear, audible voice and pronounce the lyrics carefully, so everyone can understand the song. Performers also sing with emotion and sincerity to demonstrate they understand the meaning of each phrase and line. Many country performers sing in an accent associated with the speech of the Southern Dixie States. For example, the high-pitched nasal accent spoken in the Appalachian Mountains became a prime feature of the vocal styles of artists Bill Monroe, Loretta Lynn, and Dolly Parton.

A band usually accompanies country vocalists. Some singers, however, choose to perform alone and provide their own accompaniment, usually on acoustic guitar.

The instruments used in country music differ with each style, but stringed instruments are common to almost all country groups. The stringed instruments that made up the basic ensemble of early country music were the fiddle from England, the guitar from Spain, the banjo from West Africa, and the mandolin from Italy.

As the country style came under the influence of other types of music, additional instruments were added. They included the piano, the double bass, drums, the Hawaiian steel guitar, and brass and reed instruments. Country musicians first began playing electrically amplified instruments in the 1930s.

Country music is performed in a variety of idioms. The subcategories of country music often use different sets of musical instruments and each idiom is characterized by its own approach to singing. The country genre began in the 1920s with string bands, which usually consisted of various combinations of fiddle, guitar, mandolin, banjo, and string bass, also known as a double bass. The drum set became part of country music in the 30s. Although brass wind instruments such as the trumpet and saxophone were an important part of Western swing, they are rarely heard on other country recordings.

The piano can be found on country records as early as the mid-20s, but it did not become a lead instrument until the late 1940s, with the boogie-woogie recordings of singer-composer Aubrey "Moon" Mullican. The high-pitched sound of the steel guitar made its recording debut in 1954 with the hit *Slowly* by Webb Pierce. Modern country bands usually feature at least six musicians, including a keyboardist, an electric bass player, a steel guitarist, electric and acoustic guitarists, a drummer, and an all-purpose musician who plays harmonica, fiddle, banjo, mandolin, and other instruments, as needed.

Old-time or "old-timey" music is the earliest and most traditional style of country music. It refers to the basic string bands that were common when country music was first recorded in the 1920s. The string band repertoire consisted mostly of traditional folk and gospel music and appealed mainly to people in the rural Southeast. The most common instruments in old-time bands were the guitar, fiddle, and banjo. Many old-time tunes are folk songs drawn from the roots of country music. In the 20s and 30s, such groups as the Skillet Lickers and the Stoneman Family performed in old-timey style. In the 1960s, a group called the New Lost City Ramblers revived old-timey music. In recent years the Red Clay Ramblers have carried on this rich musical tradition. Old-timey music was ushered into the twenty-first century in a big way when featured in the musical score of the film *O Brother, Where Art Thou?*

Cajun music appeared in southern Louisiana during the late nineteenth and early twentieth century. The term Cajun refers to French-speaking people from Canada who settled in Louisiana and Texas following the infamous Acadian deportation of 1755. The basic instruments in Cajun groups are the accordion and fiddle. Cajun combos also use guitars, triangles, and drums. Most Cajun tunes are sung in French and the music is frequently used to accompany dancing. Well-known Cajun performers included composer, fiddler, and vocalist Dennis McGee in the 1920s, the Hackberry Ramblers during the 30s, and Harry Choates during the 40s. The 60s folk music revival sparked interest in the Cajun style and its musicians. More recently, artists such as accordionist Marc Savoy, Zachary Richard, Steve Riley & the Mamou Playboys, and the group Beausoleil have risen to prominence.

Zydeco music, a blues flavored offshoot of Cajun, was performed by black Louisiana musicians. The King of Zydeco, Clifton Shenire, pioneered the modern form. The key instrument of both Cajun and

Zydeco, the accordion, is also prominent in the roots musical style called Tejano or Tex-Mex. Mexican-Americans living in the southern part of Texas developed Tejano music. Flaco Jiménez remains the best-known Tejano accordion player.

In the 1920s, the recording industry helped spread and popularize country music. In 1922 the first country recordings appeared, introducing the music of string bands or old-time music. The recordings were marketed as hillbilly music, partly because of a popular band called the Hill Billies. During the 20s the audience for hillbilly music expanded with the spread of small-town radio stations. The new ability of radio broadcasting to reach rural communities aided the dissemination of new musical styles, notably country music. Powerful radio stations broadcast country music around North America. With the wider distribution of music over radio, new local styles were incorporated into the gospel and folk core of the traditional country sound.

When country music was first recorded, musicians performed popular songs like *The Baggage Coach Ahead* along with folk and blues songs. Vernon Dalhart, one of country music's first recording stars, began his career as a popular singer with training in classic opera. Dalhart lived in the Northern United States and recorded in New York City. One of his hit records had a bona fide folk tune, *The Wreck of Old 97*, on one side and a sentimental popular number, *The Prisoner's Song*, on the flip side. Ever since that time, country music has been strongly affected by mainstream popular music. This influence has occurred despite the vehement objection of some fans and artists who feel that country music loses its rural, Southern identity when it sounds too much like popular music.

Country became available on records about the same time that country music radio shows appeared. Most record companies were located in the city of New York. Some country performers traveled north to record in Manhattan studios. The first country recording, Eck Robertson's version of the old-time fiddle tune *Sallie Goodin*, was recorded in New York in 1922. The rapid development of radio and the recording industry transformed country from an informal folk art into part of North America's entertainment industry. Records permitted musicians to hear a performance again and again to study lyrics and method of playing. In 1924, Chicago radio station WLS began broadcasting a live program of farce and country music. The program was later called the National Barn Dance. In 1925, WSM in Nashville began a similar radio program called the WSM Barn Dance. Station manager George D. Hay was hired from WLS to host this program, which he renamed the Grand Ole Opry in 1927. One of the program's first stars was all-round musical entertainer "Uncle" Dave Macon. Another was talented black musician DeFord Bailey.

During the 1920s and 30s, live country radio programs broadcast from many North American cities. Each country music radio show ran for several hours, usually a few nights each week. The shows featured fiddlers, guitar and piano soloists, and string bands, as well as rural poets and comedians. All the shows included ads for products of interest to folks living in rural areas. Most programs were performed in front of a live theater or studio audience. The radio stations emitted powerful signals and no other station was allowed to broadcast on their assigned frequencies. Therefore, the shows could be heard and enjoyed many miles from their station of origin. Nashville's *Grand Ole Opry*, for example, could be heard from Florida to southeastern Canada.

Radio programs provided jobs for country singers and their bands and permitted them to be heard across the continent. By singing their latest recording, artists could stimulate record sales and promote concert ticket sales by informing listeners where and when they would be appearing in concert.

In the early 1920s the traditional string-band music of the Southern mountain regions began to be commercially recorded, with Fiddlin' John Carson garnering the genre's first hit record in 1923. The realism of the rural tunes, many lyrics of which were stern and impersonal narratives of tragedies, stood in marked contrast to the often over-sentimentality of much of the pop music of the day.

Occasionally record producers traveled to the South on field trips to record music. Producers set up temporary studios and used portable recording equipment. Arthur E. Satherley and Ralph Peer were record producers from New York who pioneered field recording of country music. Peer, who was the first to record John Carson, discovered the Carter Family and Jimmie Rodgers at a 1927 field recording session in Bristol, a border town shared by the states of Tennessee and Virginia. These famous recording became known as the "Bristol sessions".

The Carter Family, a trio from rural Virginia, and the blues-oriented singer-composer Jimmie Rodgers, from Mississippi, were early country artists of importance and often credited as the creators of commercial country music. Their recorded performances strongly influenced generations of later musicians.

From the late 1920s to the early 40s the Carter trio recorded old folk ballads and country-dance tunes, incorporating such instruments as the fiddle, guitar, banjo, and Autoharp. Other instruments occasionally used by them included harmonica, mandolin, and Appalachian dulcimer, a stringed instrument with an elliptical body, a fretted fingerboard, and three strings. Vocals were done either by a single voice or in high close harmony. Whereas the vocals in early folk and hillbilly music were usually of secondary importance compared with the instrumentals, the Carter Family used their instruments to provide a musical accompaniment that never overshadowed the simple harmonies of their vocal work. The trio kept the folk tradition alive by recording tunes such as *Will the Circle Be Unbroken* and *Wildwood Flower*.

Jimmie Rodgers, who recorded over 120 songs during the late 1920s and early 30s, brought both blues and folk elements to country music through maudlin ballads and his so-called blue yodels, which introduced yodeling to a mainstream audience.

Country music continued to grow in popularity during the Great Depression. With radio and records, country musicians could listen to jazz, Hollywood film music, and other types of music that were popular beyond the rural South. Country artists and songwriters soon began to incorporate these styles into their music. As a result, several important styles of country music developed during the 1930s. Country radio programs provided free entertainment that helped folks through the hard times. This free music, however, hurt record sales, which plummeted by ninety percent in 1932, compared to 1922. In response, record companies offered inexpensive country recordings so financially strapped fans could continue to buy records.

With the migration of many Southern rural whites to industrial cities caused by the economic dislocation of the Depression, country music was brought into new territories and exposed to new influences, such as blues and gospel music. The traditional nostalgic roots of country, with its lyrics about poverty, orphans, sentimental lovers, and home-sick workers, held special appeal during a time of grinding economic hardships and wide-scale population shifts.

During this same period, virtuoso mandolin player Bill Monroe and his string band, the Blue Grass Boys, made a concerted effort to recover some of country music's root values and heritage. Kentucky native, Monroe discarded more recently adopted instruments and rhythms and brought back high harmony singing and the lead fiddle. His style combined traditional folk ballads, roots and rural music, and gospel songs with string-band music played at breakneck tempos. Alan Lomax called it "folk music in overdrive", while others described it as the "high lonesome sound".

By the mid-1940s, Bill Monroe had experimented considerably with new methods of presenting string-band music. He began to evolve a highly distinctive mandolin style while playing with his brothers Birch and Charlie. It was after their group broke up that he formed his own band. Together they already showed many of the distinctive qualities of modern bluegrass when in 1946 banjoist Earl Scruggs developed a brilliant revolutionary three-finger picking technique that brought the instrument into a lead position. Their music, with its driving, syncopated rhythms and instrumental virtuosity, took the name "bluegrass" from Monroe's band.

The seeds of Bluegrass music were planted in rural Kentucky during the 1920s and 30s. It represented, primarily through its instrumentation, a return to the prerecording days of folk music. Bluegrass bands generally feature guitar, fiddle, mandolin, banjo, bass, and an amplified steel resonator guitar called a Dobro – also known as the Hawaiian guitar because it can be played Hawaiian style by laying it across the lap. Although Bluegrass music remains faithful to the folk roots of country music, it features elaborate and complex instrumental and vocal solos accompanied by intricate harmony singing. Bluegrass artists often sing in a high-pitched, nasal style characteristic of the speech in Appalachia.

Traditional square-dance tunes, time-honored religious songs, and age-old ballads furnish a large part of the bluegrass repertory. Bluegrass standards also include perennial favorites *Orange Blossom Special* and *Blue Moon of Kentucky*.

When Bill Monroe formed the Blue Grass Boys in 1939, it marked the birth of bluegrass music. He and his band performed from the mid-20s until his death in 1996. Monroe is considered the father of bluegrass music. The bluegrass style emerged fully by the late 40s, when several groups were playing the music. The musicians who led these groups had at one time or another played with the Blue Grass Boys and learned the style from Monroe himself. One such well-known alumni was Vasser Clemens, considered the Miles Davis of the fiddle. Combining jazz with country, Clements became one of the most distinctive and inventive fiddlers in bluegrass music. He first came to prominence as a member of Monroe's band in the early 1950s, but never limited himself to traditional bluegrass. Over the next half century, he distinguished himself by incorporating several different genres into his style. In the process, he became not only one of the most respected fiddlers in bluegrass, he also became a sought-after session musician, playing with artists as diverse as Hank Williams Sr, the Monkees, Paul McCartney, Michelle Shocked, and Bonnie Raitt.

Bluegrass performances spread like wildflower on the radio in small Southern towns in the 1940s. It then moved on to television and "hillbilly" bars in the 50s, to college concerts, coffeehouses, and folk festivals in the 60s, and in the 70s the influx of younger musicians interested in bluegrass even brought some influence from rock music.

Lester Flatt was an important bluegrass artist for decades following WWII. Flatt joined Earl Scruggs to form the popular band Flatt and Scruggs. Together they expanded the bluegrass fan base and helped expose bluegrass to the masses during the folk revival of the 1960s. They appeared at the Newport Folk Festival, on the Beverly Hillbillies television show, and were featured on the musical soundtrack of the Hollywood landmark film *Bonnie and Clyde*.

The Osborne Brothers, a duo from Kentucky, were highly regarded for their work during the 1950s and 60s. Among their most notable achievements are their pioneering, inventive use of amplification, twin harmony banjos, steel guitars, and drums – they were the first bluegrass band to expand the style's sonic palette in such a way. During this same period, Arthel "Doc" Watson, who had accompanied roots music legend Clarence Ashley, became a renowned and influential acoustic guitar stylist. More recently, Ricky Skaggs, Vince Gill, Alison Krauss and her band Union Station, the Nashville Bluegrass Band, Bela Fleck & the Flecktones, The Whites, and many other young performers, have proudly carried on the traditions of bluegrass music. Others like Marty Stuart, one of the best country instrumentalists, bridge the strong traditional bluegrass and gospel past of country music with the new rockabilly, Southern Rock, contemporary sound.

The first truly urban form of country, honky-tonk music originated and developed in Alabama, Oklahoma, and the lone star state of Texas in the 1930s, 40s and early 50s. This style took its name from the working-class roadside bars and nightclubs called honky-tonks, where the music was first performed and heard by an appreciative audience. Honky-tonk music was louder and had a stronger beat than other types of country music. Honky-tonk groups expanded the role and importance of amplified instruments in country music. Most honky-tonk singers write their own tunes. Generally, these songs tell melancholy stories about life, love and romance. Another popular theme deals with the daily hardships one faces and how life's difficulties lead people to escape through drinking.

Honky-tonk's fiddle-steel-guitar combination and its resentful, sad lyrics about rural whites adrift in the big city were widely adopted by other country performers. Honky-tonk combined the maudlin ballads of folk music and older forms of country music with driving, up-tempo rhythms and the improvisational freedom of jazz music. Drums and both steel and electric guitars were prominently featured. The new style developed as a result of several factors, including the urbanization of the rural South by a hardened population scarred by WWII, the introduction of electric guitars, and a more lenient public attitude toward alcohol following the end of prohibition in 1933. Honky-tonk broadened the range of country lyrics, and tunes about drinking, marital infidelity, and divorce became nation-wide hits for the first time.

The best-known early honky-tonk stars included Texan Al Dexter and Ernest Tubb. Dexter's *Honky Tonk Blues* of 1936 was the first song to use the term honky-tonk. Tubb's 1941 honky-tonk single *Walking the Floor Over You* eventually sold more than one million records. Hank Williams Sr combined honky-tonk, blues, and more traditional country singing in his many hit songs like *Cold, Cold Heart* of 1951, *Jambalaya* of 1952 and *Your Cheatin' Heart* of 1953. Another early honky-tonk performer was singer-songwriter Lefty Frizzell, whose innovative singing style greatly influenced later vocalists such as George Jones and Merle Haggard. The high standards set by early honky-tonk pioneers were passed on to modern country superstars including Randy Travis, Alan Jackson, Dwight Yoakam, Garth Brooks, and the duo of Brooks & Dunn.

During the 1930s and 40s movies about cowboys and the American West popularized the style known as cowboy or Western music. Cowboy music became popular in the 1930s and 40s, when singing cowboy Hollywood films were produced. Ken Maynard, Tex Ritter, Roy Rogers, and Gene Autry, all had careers as country singers in addition to starring roles in cowboy films. Autry, who had appeared on the *National Barn Dance* radio program, made his first singing cowboy film in 1935. Rogers was an original member of the Sons of the Pioneers, a band that appeared in 85 Westerns. The group's style of three-part harmony singing became broadly popular and influential.

Most of the tunes in these movies described pioneering life in the Western United States. The singers were accompanied by guitar, harmonica, accordion, or fiddle. Professional songwriters from New York City and Hollywood wrote most of these movie tunes.

The Western style eventually grew beyond its stereotypical use in cowboy movies. Originally, Western music grew out of a nineteenth century tradition of cowboy songs and string bands that was particularly strong in Oklahoma, Arkansas and Texas. Modern western music often features improvisation and a wide range of instruments, including wind instruments. The lyrics, however, still center around folklore life on the Western frontier, and, the romanticized cowboy of the late 1800s.

A variation on traditional Western music called "Western swing" developed in Oklahoma and Texas during the 1920s and 30s. Western swing was a country rendition of the big-band jazz music popular during the 30s and 40s. Western swing bands combined the traditional string band with instruments commonly used in blues and jazz. They featured the fiddle, conventional guitar, and steel guitar, alongside trumpets, saxophones, piano, and drums.

Milton Brown led popular Western swing bands in the 1930s and 40s. The style also gained fame through fiddler Bob Wills and His Texas Playboys, a band that included almost twenty musicians. Wills began recording Western swing music in 1935 and was a top musical attraction throughout the Southwest during the 40s and 50s. His innovative fiddling style and musical arrangements had a central influence on later country acts, including singers Buck Owens, Willie Nelson, George Strait, and the band Asleep at the Wheel.

The Second World War produced changes in North American society that had an impact on country music. During the war, many rural Southerners left their farms to move close to factories in big urban centers. In addition, Southern men traveled overseas with the military forces. These transplanted Southerners brought with them their records and love for country music. As a result, the taste for country music expanded outside the Southern United States.

The economic surge that followed WWII expanded the opportunities for the entertainment industry, including country music recordings and performances. The post war economic boom favored the emergence of the country music industry beyond its former geographical borders. Radio exposed a broader audience to country music while new, relatively inexpensive recording technology made records available at affordable prices. These forces helped create demand for country recordings in greater variety and quantity than ever before. Country music began to reflect its changed audience.

One of the most successful responses to this new demand for country music was the style called "rockabilly". Rockabilly music emerged in the mid-1950s on the rhythmic banks of the mighty Mississippi river in the city of Memphis. An early form of rock and roll, rockabilly was a blend of white hillbilly music and black R&B. Performed at faster tempos than other country styles, rockabilly bands often featured an acoustic rhythm guitar, piano, drums, a stand up bass, as well as an electric guitar played with a twang. Rockabilly vocals emphasize rhythmic phrases and unconventional singing with high-pitched whines, quick yelps, and other unusual nuances.

Rockabilly music had close ties to traditional country music. County legend Johnny Cash began his career as a rockabilly artist. Elvis Presley, Carl Perkins, and rocking pianist Jerry Lee Lewis, were major rockabilly entertainers. These performers took fans away from more traditional honky-tonk and bluegrass artists. Memphis record producer Sam Philips pioneered rockabilly on his small Sun Records label. During the early 1950s, Phillips began recording black blues artists from Memphis such as Junior Parker, Rosco Gordon, Ike Turner, and Rufus Thomas who launched his recording career with a song called *Bear Cat*. Written as an "answer song" to Big Mama Thornton's hit *Hound Dog, Bear Cat* brought Sun its first real taste of success. During the mid-50s Phillips turned his attention to rockabilly music and was the first to record Cash, Perkins, Lewis, and Presley. Many recent country performers, including singer Mark Collie and successful group the Mavericks, have been influenced by rockabilly.

During the 1940s, Nashville began to emerge as a center for country music. The *Grand Ole Opry*, now broadcast across North America on the NBC radio network, became the most important country music radio show, and country music publishing became an important Nashville business. Singer and fiddle player Roy Acuff, who joined the *Opry* in 1938, was its brightest star in the 40s and 50s. In 1942, Acuff and songwriter Fred Rose formed Acuff-Rose Publishing in Nashville, the first publishing house for country music. In 1946, Acuff-Rose signed Hank Williams Sr as a songwriter. Williams made hit recordings of his own tunes, and several of his songs were also hits when later recorded by pop artists. Though Hank Williams Sr died in 1953 when he was only 29 years old, many country music aficionados consider him to be the most influential artist in country music history.

The meteoric rise to fame of Hank William Sr in the late 1940s also helped establish Nashville as the undisputed center for the production of country music. The city offered large recording studios, the Grand Ole Opry as a first-class concert venue, and the WSM nationwide radiobroadcast program. Soon after WWII, WSM employees founded one of the first Nashville recording studios, Castle Studios. In 1949 Sun Records built its recording studio in nearby Memphis. In 1952 musicians Owen and Harold Bradley set up Bradley Recording, one of the first independent recording studios in downtown Nashville. The Bradley brothers recorded country stars Kitty Wells, Ernest Tubb, Patsy Cline, and rock and roll pioneer Buddy Holly. The commercial success of the Bradleys helped convince major record companies to build studios in Nashville. By the late 1950s numerous country performers, songwriters, and studio musicians had relocated to "Music City, USA" as Nashville came to be known.

In the mid-1950s, rock and roll emerged and captured much of the country music audience. For the remainder of the decade, Nashville confronted this crisis and tried to regain the fans it had lost. To increase the exposure of country music, record companies and radio stations assertively promoted country performers and songwriters. The Country Music Association aka CMA was chartered in Nashville in 1958 to promote country music. The CMA organized concerts in big cities and initiated an annual country music awards show. In 1961 the Country Music Hall of Fame was founded in Nashville to commemorate the individuals who have made the most important contributions to country music.

During the late 1950s and early 60s, Nashville executives and record producers Billy Sherrill, Chet Atkins, and Owen Bradley, created and shaped the Nashville sound. This new style had a broad commercial appeal by incorporating modern pop music arrangements with full and smooth vocals, violin sections, and background choruses. The Nashville sound was an attempt to attract a wider audience by combining elements of rock, pop, and country music. Although it featured country songs performed by country stars, the Nashville sound was produced with the technology and expertise of popular music of the period. For example, full orchestral string sections often replaced traditional mandolin, fiddle, and guitar ensembles to create a rich accompaniment. A chorus of backup singers filled out the vocal tracks of a song. The use of synthesizers, reverb effects, overdubbing, and other studio techniques helped fashion a more marketable and modern sound.

A small pool of gifted instrumentalists, called session musicians, played on nearly all country records waxed in Nashville during this period. These musicians developed a relaxed approach to performing that did not require written music. Guitarist Chet Atkins and pianist Floyd Cramer were influential session musicians.

Recording artists associated with this sophisticated style included Jim Reeves, Porter Wagoner, Eddy Arnold, Tammy Wynette, Buck Owens, Patsy Cline, Lee Greenwood, Kenny Rogers, Loretta Lynn, the Gatlin Brothers, Charley Pride, and Barbara Mandrell. Every one of these Nashville singers cut songs that were hits with both country and pop fans. Such recordings were called "crossover" hits, because they crossed over from one type of music to another. Rogers's *She Believes in Me*, Arnold's *Make the World Go Away*, and Cline's *Crazy*, were major crossover hits in the Nashville sound style.

By 1965, country music had regained much of the audience it had lost to other pop styles, and had attracted new fans. The marketing work of the CMA, the popularity of the *Grand Ole Opry*, and the Nashville sound reinvigorated country music with renewed success.

The 1960s were years of expansion and prosperity for the country music industry. Many new recording studios and record companies were opened. Nashville continued to dominate as a center for country music songwriting, publishing, and recording. During the late 60s, most country recordings contained elements of the Nashville sound. Only Bakersfield, California, home to Buck Owens and Merle Haggard, competed with Nashville as a hub for country music songwriting and recording.

During the 1970s the major-label, big-studio approach remained part of the country music industry, as did the overall tendency to combine country and pop music into a style referred to as "country pop". Several mainstream pop music artists, including Olivia Newton-John and John Denver, made successful recordings of country songs. Conversely, other so-called crossover artists combined popular and country styles to achieve mainstream success, often through remakes of earlier pop hits. This category of country stars included Glen Campbell, Kenny Rogers, Dolly Parton, Conway Twitty, Tanya Tucker, Barbara Mandrell, Lynn Anderson, and Lee Greenwood,

By the mid-1970s, many in the country music industry had

grown tired of the Nashville sound. The same session musicians played on most recordings, and some felt that their work was stagnant and no longer creative. Many country fans, critics and artists believed that Nashville music had become too similar to mainstream pop music.

In response to this reality, country music once again adapted to the times and its audience. Country and rock music had borrowed from one another since the late 1950s. In fact, many early rock music performers began their careers in country music. Rock and roll, the earliest form of rock music, borrowed musical elements from the hillbilly style and Western swing. During the late 60s and 70s the Byrds, Buffalo Springfield, Poco, the Eagles, Gram Parsons, Willie Nelson, Linda Ronstadt, Bob Dylan, Roy Orbison, and other performers began to combine elements of rock and country in their music. The resulting idiom, known as "country rock", fuses country and rock styles by taking country melody, harmony, and lyric themes and adding the driving percussive beat, rhythms, and electric instrumentation of rock. The most popular country rock band of the last few decades was Alabama.

The so-called "outlaw country" movement developed parallel to country rock. It emerged in the mid-1970s in reaction against the Nashville sound and the record labels that had institutionalized the Nashville style. The gap between country and the mainstream of pop music continued to narrow as electric guitars replaced more traditional country instruments. Some acts rejected the conservative Nashville sound and sought to break away from the generic recording formulas that by the 70s dominated the industry. These performers wanted more control over the recording process, and many of them opined for a return to the acoustic instruments, small ensembles, and natural-sounding vocals of country music's heritage. Early exponents of outlaw country included the prominent Nashville expatriate artists Waylon Jennings, Willie Nelson, the Glaser Brothers, Merle Haggard, Johnny Cash, Kris Kristofferson, and David Allan Coe. These singers and songwriters were called outlaws. The outlaws often recorded with members of their touring bands rather than with session musicians. More importantly, the outlaws returned to earlier, more traditional styles of country music. Together, they embodied this spirit of rebellion through their music and their behavior, dressing down in tattered blue jeans and T-shirts and using illegal drugs. As country musicians moved away from Nashville, smaller, independent recording studios and labels were started in Austin, Texas, Bakersfield, and other cities. Many outlaws, including Nelson and Jennings, performed in honky-tonk style.

Others, like Emmylou Harris, performed in an updated bluegrass style.

The major country labels at first refused to support outlaw country music. As radio coverage and concerts popularized the music of outlaw performers, impressive record sales eventually convinced these labels to allow their acts to produce or co-produce their own records. In 1976 the album *Wanted – The Outlaws*, a compilation of tunes from Nelson, Jennings, Tompall Glaser, and Jessi Colter, became country's first platinum-selling album, selling more than one million copies in the United States. Contemporary artists such as Steve Earle, Travis Tritt, and Dwight Yoakam have adopted the outlaw style.

The outlaws began a process of change in country music that eventually led to yet another variation called "new country". In the late 1980s and early 90s, a number of young country artists came to prominence who had been influenced by the outlaws. These artists were called "new traditionalists". They rejected musical influences that had made country music sound like popular music and returned to the styles of earlier years.

Many new traditionalists drew upon the honky-tonk, or "hard-country," style of Hank Williams Sr and other honky-tonk performers of the 1950s. Hank Williams Jr became one of the few to develop a musical career that was not only successful, but also markedly different from his legendary father. Originally, Hank Junior simply copied and played his father's music, but as he grew older, he began to carve out his own niche and it was one that owed as much to country rock as it did to honky-tonk. In the late 70s, he reshaped his image to appeal both to outlaw country fans and rowdy Southern rockers, and his makeover worked, resulting in a string of top ten singles. Other popular outlaw country and Southern country rock artists include Charlie Daniels and Lynyrd Skynyrd.

The term new country dates from the mid-1980s when a handful of new traditionalists, notably John Anderson, Randy Travis, Ricky Skaggs, Dwight Yoakam, Alan Jackson, and the Brooks & Dunn duo, led yet another return to the sounds of traditional country music. This return was first and foremost to such instruments as steel guitars and single or twin fiddles, as opposed to full orchestral string sections. One of the most popular new traditionalists was singer-songwriter Garth Brooks. Despite new country's original modest and humble intentions, Brooks achieved his dramatic success with radio, recordings, and live performances in part by finding and writing songs that were extremely well received as well as adding elements of stadium rock productions to his elaborate stage shows. In 1990 his second album, *No Fences*, became the top-selling country music album of all time. Brooks wrote realistic songs about everyday life and delivered them in a honky-tonk singing style. Some of his hits, such as *The Thunder Rolls* and *We Shall Be Free*, dealt with social and political issues. Like Brooks, many country artists of the 1990s combined styles from country music's past with music videos and modern stage productions. A decade after the term new country was coined to indicate a return to country's roots; it was applied to all new performers in country music, regardless of their style. As a result, country music had more fans and sold more records in the mid-1990s than at any other time in its history.

In the late 1980s Clint Black, another new-country performer, introduced an era of so-called "hat acts". Following Black's example, nearly all male country singers began wearing Stetson cowboy hats, symbolizing the return of country to its rural roots and heritage.

New country also prominently featured female performers, including Patty Loveless, Reba McEntire, Shania Twain, Trisha Yearwood, Mary Chapin Carpenter, Wynonna, Leann Rimes, Faith Hill, and the Dixie Chicks – to name a few. During the first half of the twentieth century country music offered few opportunities for women. They usually occupied backup singing or musician roles and were often filled by women married or closely related to another band member. Patsy Montana was the first woman to have a commercially successful solo career in country music. Her 1935 recording *I Want to be a Cowboy's Sweetheart* became the first country recording by a woman to sell more than one million copies and gave women a new, more powerful image in the industry. Singer-songwriter and honky-tonk "angel" Kitty Wells composed songs addressing such social problems as drinking and divorce. Wells hit it big with her 1952 single *It Wasn't God Who Made Honky Tonk Angels*. The song represented a woman's response to the rambunctious bad-boy life commonly glorified and celebrated in the music of male country vocalists. It was the first song by a female country artist to hit the top of the country music charts. Later in her career, Kitty Wells was belovedly known as the "Queen of Country Music". Her accomplishments paved the way for subsequent generations of female country music singers.

The 1960s, and later the 70s and 80s, brought new prominence to the role of women in country music. Patsy Cline, Loretta Lynn, Tammy Wynette, and Dolly Parton enjoyed commercial success singing and composing both country and pop music. The 1980 film

110

Coal Miner's Daughter depicted how Lynn surmounted the severe poverty of her early life to become the first millionaire among female country performers and the first woman named entertainer of the year by the CMA. Dolly Parton's hit composition *I Will Always Love You* was later covered by pop diva Whitney Houston, making it one of the biggest mainstream hits of all-time. Also popular during this period were prominent female country singers such as Tanya Tucker, Crystal Gayle, and Reba McEntire. By the mid-90s McEntire had crossed another threshold for women in the industry by conquering the business end, establishing herself in the publishing, managerial, and recording studio areas of country music.

The average age of country performers began falling in the mid-1980s, partly explained by the rise of music video as a prime promotional tool. While still showcasing musical abilities, labels often placed greater importance on the looks and sex appeal of performers. During the early 90s, North American sales of country music tripled in volume. In addition, country music made important advances overseas. Country Music Television, a 24-hour cable television channel, commenced a period of ambitious foreign expansion in the 90s and by 1997 was available via cable or satellite around the globe.

Country music has developed a broad spectrum of styles and attracted a large mainstream audience by adapting elements of other musical styles. For example, since the 1930s, folk and country styles have continued to influence one another. Major figures of folk country music included Johnny Cash beginning in the 1960s, and recent country artists Lyle Lovett, the Judds, and Mary Chapin Carpenter.

Many country recordings of the 1990s would have been classified as pop or rock records in past years. As in many periods since country music first emerged, in the late 90s a group of artists encouraged a return to a simple, unpretentious country style. This movement, known as "Countrypolitan", "Americana", "Alternative Country", or Neo-Traditionalist Country", gained exposure and momentum through college and public radio stations and concerts across the USA. Americana underscored individual performers who combined singing, musicianship, and songwriting. It encompassed musicians who were new to the industry, such as the band BR5-49 and singer-guitarist Robbie Fulks – who became one of the more important members of Chicago's new country music scene – as well as established artists Nanci Griffith, Guy Clark, Jerry Jeff Walker, and Johnny Cash. With a career that spanned six decades, Johnny Cash was part of the birth of rock and roll and went on to reach the pinnacle of country music. His music, perhaps more than any other recording artist's, captures the struggle, joy, tragedy, and ultimate redemption of the common man. Shortly before his death in 2003 "The Man in Black" received an MTV award for his last recordings. Cash's wife, country-star June Carter Cash, was part of the Carter Family legacy.

Country music tends to reflect the concerns, achievements, and lifestyle of the times, and remains an important form of North American cultural expression. Western-style clothing and numerous catch phrases from country songs have found their way into North American lexicon and pop culture. Although country music was born in the politically conservative and patriotic American South, its audience and many of its artists come from all parts of the political dial. At times, country songs have stirred controversy by broaching troubling domestic issues. Perhaps the main quality of country music and the source of its lasting appeal and popularity are its simplicity and direct observations on the everyday issues and concerns of its fans.

Since the terrorist attacks on September 11th 2001, country music responded quickly, appealing to the patriotism of its fan-base. In some county music quarters there developed a strong vein of patriotism. The horrors of 911 prompted some country artists to express overt and sometimes blatant American patriotism in their songs, touching a nerve amongst many grass-roots country fans. The tremendous success of singer-songwriter Toby Keith best exemplifies this new lyrical approach with his hit song *Courtesy of the Red, White and Blue (The Angry American)*.

Over the decades, country music has evolved into one of the most important divisions of the North American music industry. It retains its vitality and has become more acceptable to a national urban audience. As the twenty-first century gathers steam, country music has become more popular than at any other time in its rich history. Despite its embrace of other popular styles, country music retains an unmistakable character as one of the few truly indigenous North American musical styles.

clockwise from top left: Diana Ross & The Supremes,
Stevie Wonder, The Temptations, Smokey Robinson

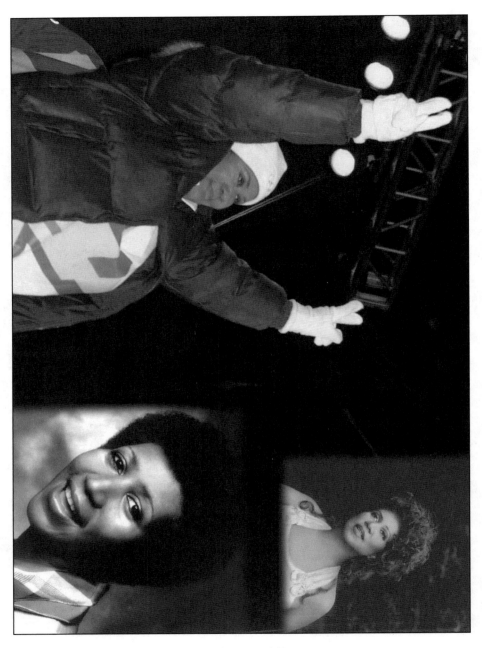

Aretha Franklin

top: Whitney Houston
bottom: Mariah Carey

Prince

6.   R&B

R&B or rhythm and blues music has come to denote a variety of different, but related, types of pop music produced and supported primarily by African American urban musicians beginning in the early 1940s. R&B music embraces such genres as jump and club blues, black rock and roll, doo-wop, soul, Motown, funk, disco, and rap.

The expression rhythm-and-blues was first used in 1949 by future Atlantic record executive Jerry Wexler. It began as a replacement for "race records", the music-industry term for records made by black musicians for black audiences. The term rhythm and blues then was used as a synonym for black rock and roll in the early and mid-50s. Until white rock and roll performers achieved popularity, what was called rock and roll by white fans and disc jockeys, or "DJs", was referred to as the latest style of R&B by black fans and DJs.

R&B has provided a great influence on pop music worldwide. This influence can be traced in forms of jazz, country, gospel, worldbeat, and rock music. As the impact of various styles of R&B has expanded, African American urban values have also permeated a wide variety of other cultures, most notably that of contemporary white North America.

Despite important differences, there are common musical and social elements that link the many genres of R&B. Musical rhythm is the key distinguishing trademark of R&B music and its sub styles. The primary means of differentiating one style from another, and even one musician or band from another is the distinguishing employment of a "backbeat", "groove" and "timbre". The backbeat consists of emphasizing the second and fourth beats of each measure, while the groove denotes the specific approach to the expression of musical time. Timbre refers to the color or quality of a sound. For example, a listener may tell one kind of instrument apart from another, or distinguish one singer from another, by the differences in their timbre. Most styles of R&B rely on timbre variation over the course of a performance to achieve interest. R&B vocalists and musicians often alternate between smooth, velvety timbres and coarse, raspy timbres, giving the music a wide range of emotional expression.

In addition to rhythm and timbre, other common elements of

R&B music include the use of basic blues structure, call-and-response, constant repetition of musical notes, rhythms, phrases, or verses, the use of blue notes (notes that bridge the musical relationship between the minor and major modes), and a complex and integrated blending of instruments, in which it is sometimes a challenge to differentiate the separate instruments or sounds being played.

Most R&B performances share a common instrumentation, with the band divided into a rhythm section and a brass or horn section. Usually, the rhythm section consists of drums, guitar, piano and/or organ, and bass, while the brass section features trumpets, saxophones, and trombones. The importance of horns in most styles of R&B has been one of the key ways in which R&B has been traditionally differentiated from white rock music.

R&B originated from the changes that took place in North America just prior to and during WWII. Foremost among the sociological, industrial, and technological changes was a widespread shift in demographics. New farming machinery replaced manual labor on cotton and tobacco farms in America's Deep South. Lured by relatively high-paying wartime employment, hundreds of thousands of African Americans migrated from the rural South to Northeast, Midwest, and West Coast urban centers. In pop music, new idioms were fashioned to meet the evolving tastes of this demographic group, leading to the development of the urbane sounds of R&B. By the 1950s, the migration of America's blacks to northern cities had resulted in the cross-fertilization of the forms and vocal styles of blues with the up-tempo rhythms of jazz to create R&B.

The significant sociological changes of the WWII period were accompanied by several important technological developments, including the invention of the electric guitar in the late 1930s and the tape recorder, discovered at the end of the war in Germany hands. With the new, relatively affordable technology of magnetic tape, which simplified the recording process, enterprising individuals were able to start small independent record labels. Since most of the major record companies in North America had little interest in R&B, newly formed independent labels, such as Modern, Atlantic, Chess, and Specialty, were crucial for the production and distribution of blues and R&B records.

Another important industrial change resulted from the rise of television broadcasting in North America in the late 1940s. Radio-station owners, believing that television would soon make radio obsolete, sold their stations at low prices. New radio-station proprietors, searching for a niche in the marketplace, often turned to newly urbanized African Americans. Beginning with the Memphis radio station WDIA in 1948, these new black-oriented radio stations allowed the fledgling independent record labels to disseminate the sounds of R&B to an African American urban audience.

One of the pioneers of this type of early black urban music was being created and performed by a former big-band jazz singer and saxophonist called Louis Jordan. Jordon formed a band in 1938, which he eventually named the Tympany Five. He recorded primarily in the up-tempo, horn-driven style known as jump blues. His compositions were based on traditional 12-bar blues and featured simplified rhythmic solos, humorous lyrics, and riffs, commonly played by the horn section. Many of Jordan's biggest hits, including *Caldonia* of 1945 and *Choo Choo Ch'Boogie* of 1946, were exceedingly popular with both white and black urban listeners. The jump blues style he originated quickly spread among African American musicians, with regional distinctions emerging in urban centers such as New Orleans and Memphis. Jordan influenced every R&B musician in the 40s, 50s, and early 60s. His well-crafted style also helped ignite the birth of rock and roll.

In the late 1940s, when many jazz musicians began to play the rhythmically complex bebop style, black dancers turned to big bands playing a blues-derived, saxophone-dominated music with a heavy beat. It was louder, larger-scaled, and less subtle than the older blues and jazz styles, and it was soon supplemented by small sax-and-piano jump bands using boogie-woogie rhythms, country-blues bands featuring electric guitars and harmonicas, and African American teenage singing harmony groups. These new sounds led to the emergence of two new styles of R&B popular in the late 40s and early 50s. Firstly, an instrumental strain largely modeled on jump blues and featuring a coarse, honking tenor saxophone sound, and secondly, the vocal group genre. The most recognized musicians who promoted the instrumental style were alto and baritone saxophonist Paul Williams, and tenor saxophonists Big Jay McNeely and Joe Houston. The most important vocal groups of the time included the Ravens, the Mills Brothers, and the Ink Spots.

At the same time, a number of pianists, including Charles Brown and Nat "King" Cole, pioneered a much softer, subdued crooning singing style known as "club blues". By playing ballads with a highly rhythmic piano style, Cole was also able to market his music with success to both white and black consumers.

In the 1950s R&B began to be directed toward teenagers instead of adults. The vocal group style of the 40s gave way to 50s "doo-wop", which featured close-harmony singing, usually at slower tempos. Groups such as the Five Keys, and later the Drifters and the Coasters, sang tunes with lyric themes that described concerns of teenagers, including cars, rebellion, romance, and school.

Through the early 1950s, there was an increased interest in R&B by white audiences. White musicians borrowed the form, the beat, and the sound of R&B to create rock and roll music in the mid-50s. Many of the early rock hits by white performers, were R&B hits originally recorded by black artists. Some black R&B performers crossed over and became rock and roll musicians.

Pioneered largely by pianist Little Richard and guitarist Chuck Berry, black rock and roll forever changed North American culture. The crucial innovation of black rock and roll was in the expression of rhythm. Richard and Berry subdivided the basic beat that had been the hallmark of the earlier blues styles. With this innovation, an exciting, propulsive groove was achieved. Both performers also greatly increased the tempo of their performances, giving their music a frenzied style that appealed to teenagers. Finally, both artists wrote songs that reflected the youthful whims of their audience. Classics such as Little Richard's *Tutti Frutti* of 1955 and *Lucille* of 1957, and Berry's *Maybellene* of 1955 and *Johnny B. Goode* of 1958 were performed by other acts countless times in the 60s and 70s. As important as these performers were in originating a brand new style of music, trends in R&B tended to increasingly diverge from rock and roll in the early 60s.

The three most important styles of R&B during the 1960s were Chicago soul, the Motown sound, and southern soul. Chicago soul was influenced by gospel music songs and epitomized by the work of singer-songwriter Curtis Mayfield with the group the Impressions. Mayfield wrote compositions of faith and inspiration with songs such as 1965's *People Get Ready*, which featured several different lead singers trading vocal phrases in call-and-response fashion. Other characteristics of Mayfield and the Chicago soul genre included the use of falsetto, the writing of distinctive parts for stringed instruments, the use of a musical percussion instrument called the vibraphone, and a song structure that incorporated short interludes, often arranged for unique instrumental combinations such as guitar and vibes.

In 1959 Berry Gordy, Jr formed the Motown record company in Detroit, Michigan. The Motown sound combined polished songwriting with a straightforward vocal delivery and musical accompaniment and arrangements by a group of talented studio musicians called the Funk Brothers. Gordy was so successful at developing a trademark sound for Motown records that the company name soon began to be applied as a designation for a style of music. The leading Motown artists of the 60s included the female vocal group the Supremes featuring singer Diana Ross, singer and songwriter Smokey Robinson with the male vocal group the Miracles, saxophonist Junior Walker, the male singing group the Temptations, vocalists Marvin Gaye and Stevie Wonder, and one of Motown's most dependable acts Gladys Knight & the Pips. The majority of Motown artists were vocal groups that updated the doo-wop style of the 50s with a heavy, even beat. The so-called "uptown" sound of the Motown groups was created by adding lyrics about young love and well crafted orchestrations to R&B beats. Influenced by Tin Pan Alley, the compositions and arrangements were exceedingly sophisticated and the productions were elaborate, vibrant, and rich with horns and strings. Motown represented the sound of North American youth through most of the 60s and, for an independent record label, achieved unprecedented success and power in the music industry.

Others, like singer-songwriter James Brown and singer-pianist Ray Charles, combined the emotional, vocally complex style of gospel music with R&B, creating what became known as "soul music". Soul music became the most popular form of black music in the 1960s. Primarily recorded by black artists, it found wide popularity amongst both black and white audiences. Soul music developed from the harsh, emotional R&B style, but it had a smoother sound and more widely pleasing melodies. Brown and Charles originated southern soul music, the most gospel-influenced style of R&B. On many of the earliest soul records, Charles would take a traditional religious song and transform it into a secular homage to love. By adding such refinements as string accompaniments, southern soul remained an important presence in pop music throughout the 60s and much of the 70s, with such successful artists as the "king of rock and soul" Solomon Burke, the family singing group the Staple Singers, and Memphis-based vocalists Isaac Hayes and Al Green.

One of the greatest soul singers was New York-based Atlantic Records artist Aretha Franklin, singing in a style that stayed close to her gospel roots. The gritty soul styles of Sam Cooke, Otis Redding, Sam and Dave, and various artists from the Stax record label in Memphis were also popular with white and black audiences alike. Founded at the same time as Motown, Stax developed its own unique, recognizable sound with a studio band consisting of instrumental group Booker T. and the MG's, keyboardist Isaac Hayes, and the Mar-Key horn section aka Memphis Horns. With star musicians producing a light, gospel-derived sound, Stax artists sold records to white audiences while generating impressive sales among black listeners.

Black gospel music, which became distinctive by 1930, is especially associated with Pentecostal churches. A counterpoint to the blues, it developed out of the combination of the earlier hymns, black performance styles, and elements from black spirituals. Singing and lively, ecstatic dance, is usually accompanied by organ or piano, often with tambourines, enthusiastic handclapping, and electric guitars. Noted vocalists include the Golden Gate Quartet, The Clara Ward Singers, the so-called "Queen of Gospel" Mahalia Jackson, and the controversial Sister Rosetta Tharpe; who sang and played her electric guitar in churches, as well as nightclubs. Lyrics usually emphasize themes of consolation and salvation. Chicago blues musician Thomas A. Dorsey – considered the father of black gospel music – wrote many such famous lyrics including *Precious Lord*, in 1932. Although the white and black varieties of gospel music have remained different, repertoire has been shared, and they have freely influenced each other stylistically.

The Righteous Brothers weren't brothers, but Bill Medley and Bobby Hatfield inspired the term "blue-eyed soul" in the mid-1960s. The white Southern California duo were an established journeyman doo-wop/R&B act before an association with Phil Spector produced one of the most memorable hits of the sixties, *You've Lost That Lovin' Feelin'*.

At the height of soul music's popularity during the late 1960s, significant changes in cultural views began to be articulated by many African Americans. Black militancy gained momentum, accompanied by an increased sense of African heritage. This social, historical, and cultural focus on African identity was reflected in pop music. With the 1967 song *Cold Sweat*, Georgian born James Brown signaled the birth of "funk" music. Funk de-emphasized melody and harmony, bringing rhythm, the defining characteristic of black African music, to the forefront. Brown continued to showcase his idiosyncratic genre of music with such hits as *Papa's got a brand new bag, I Feel Good, Sex Machine*, and *Living In America*. Nicknamed the "hardest working man in show-business" and "the godfather of soul", James Brown invented the grooves that are still amongst the driving forces of pop music.

Named after a slang word for "stink," funk was indeed the most primal form of R&B, surpassing even Southern soul in terms of earthiness. It was also the least structured, often stretching out into extended jams, and the most Africanized, built on dynamic, highly syncopated polyrhythms. As such, it originally appealed only to hardcore R&B audiences. The groove was the most prime musical element of funk – all the instruments of the ensemble played off of one another to create it, and worked it over and over. Deep electric bass lines often served as main riffs, with an interlocking web of short, scratchy guitar chords and blaring horns over the top. Complete verses and refrains were often written without a chord change. This style was adopted by a number of performers including the group Sly and the Family Stone, who started out as a soul band influenced by rock and psychedelia. They became a full-fledged funk outfit with 1969's *Stand!* and vocalist George Clinton with the groups Parliament and Funkadelic. These musicians synthesized the funk style with elements from white rock music. Rocker Jimi Hendrix was a major inspiration for funk guitar soloists.

Disco rivaled funk's popularity in the early 1970s and ultimately surpassed it by the middle of the decade. Like funk, disco was a dance-oriented style. In contrast to funk, however, disco was dominated by arrangements laden with strings and synthesizers that tended to underscore the importance of beats one and three, often creating a heartbeat-like rhythm. Disco emerged out of gay, Latino, and black urban subcultures. The genre prominently featured female artists, such as American singers Gloria Gaynor, Tina Charles and Donna Summer. For a time, disco was even viewed as a substantial threat to mainstream rock music. Although the songs and hits were often better known than the artists, disco nevertheless managed to give rise to a handful of highly popular groups such as KC & the Sunshine Band and Earth, Wind & Fire, and a second career to the well-known pop-ballad trio, the Bee Gees.

By the mid-1970s many different sounds began to mix in R&B.

Soul continued to be popular in the early 70s, until the lighter pop music of vocal groups featuring close harmonies and falsetto singing began to dominate. Salsa added its different rhythms and instrumentation, and the thumping beats of disco music were a formularized rendition of R&B. Modified by rock sound and production values, the style continued into the 80s, led by older artists such as Smokey Robinson and Patti LaBelle.

In the 1980s and 90s disco gave way to several other dance genres. During this period, R&B artists like Prince, worked within funk and other styles of dance music and produced songs by drawing from a number of styles. Michael Jackson, in particular, was influenced by pop music from other ethnic regions, most notably Latin America. He, along with producer Quincy Jones, brought R&B to a new level of pop sophistication. Although a number of hybrid genres were created during this time, most popular R&B music remained dance-oriented. Moreover, with the rise of music video in the early 80s, the dancing abilities of artists like Jackson gained in importance. Legendary R&B artist Jackie Wilson admittedly inspired the Michael Jackson dancing style and many of Jackson's famous signature dance moves.

In the 1990s and early 2000s, the vocal group tradition of R&B continued its popularity with the quartet Boyz II Men and the trio Destiny's Child featuring Beyoncé Knowles, as did the prominence of solo vocal acts with Whitney Houston, Mariah Carey, Janet Jackson, Luther Vandross, Toni Braxton, and Brian McKnight. R&B music continues to heavily influence the evolution of modern popular music. The most recent genre of R&B is rap music. Rap is generally spoken or chanted at a fast pace rather than sung. Rap is performed over musical accompaniment that emphasizes rhythm rather than melody. Often this accompaniment consists of short segments of earlier recorded music combined in new patterns. Rap is, by far, the most important recent development in popular music and owes much to its R&B influences.

Buddy Holly, The Big Bopper, Ritchie Valens

The Beach Boys

The Rolling Stones

The Doors

Pink Floyd

David Bowie

Genesis & Phil Collins

top: Elton John
bottom: Billy Joel

top: The Ramones
bottom: Sex Pistols

Bruce Springsteen

clockwise from top left: Ozzy Osbourne, Iron Maiden,
Mötley Crüe, Slayer, Judas Priest, Metallica

Kurt Cobain of Nirvana

U2

7. ROCK

Popular music underwent a major revolution in the 1950s, as musicians combined elements of black R&B and country music to create a new genre called rock music. Rock Music is a group of related music styles that have dominated pop music in North America since about 1955. Rock originated in the United States, but its influence is now spread worldwide. It has shaped and in turn been shaped by a broad palette of cultures and musical traditions, including the blues and gospel music, classical and folk music, electronic and techno music, the worldbeat music of Africa, Asia and Latin America, and the spirit of American country music. The term "rock" commonly encompasses a variety of music styles including rock and roll, R&B, heavy metal, punk, alternative, and grunge.

Rock music is one of the world's most popular and adaptable musical forms. Rock and roll of the late 1950s relied heavily upon 12-bar blues. Some rock acts of the late 60s experimented with more flexible, open-ended forms, and some rock groups of the 70s developed forms derived from classical music.

The central musical instrument in most kinds of rock is the electric guitar. There are many important figures in the history of this instrument including jazz instrumentalist Charlie Christian, who in the late 1930s was one of the first to play the amplified guitar as a solo instrument. T-Bone Walker was the first blues musician to record with an amplified guitar in 1942. Leo Fender introduced the first mass-produced solid-body electric guitar in 1948. Les Paul popularized the instrument in the early 50s with a series of technologically innovative recordings and his 1952 endorsement of the Gibson Company's first solidbody electric guitar – The Les Paul Model. Rock and roll guitarist Chuck Berry established a style of playing in the late 50s that remains an important influence on rock music. Beginning in the late 60s a new generation of rock guitarists, including virtuosos Jimi Hendrix, Eric Clapton, and Carlos Santana, experimented with amplification, electronic sound distortion or "feedback", and various electronic devices; broadening the musical potential of the instrument.

Other instruments commonly used in rock music include the electric bass guitar, introduced by Fender in 1951, keyboard instruments such as the organ, synthesizer, acoustic and electric piano, the saxophone, and the drum set. The microphone also functions as a musical instrument for many rock vocalists, who rely upon the amplification and various effects obtainable through electronic means. The instruments played in early rock combos were modeled from the blues combos of Muddy Waters.

The first type of rock music, rock and roll, originated in the mid-1950s, and was derived from music of the American South. It arose as an amalgam of black R&B with country music, adapting the powerful rhythms and melancholy vocalizations of urban blues to a quicker tempo and an exuberant emotional tone. Rock and roll music generally followed a 4/4 beat and used only two or three chords in its melody. The tunes were simple, repetitive, and most of them were less than three minutes in length.

Rock and roll quickly attracted the attention of young people, who, with new disposable incomes resulting from higher living standards in the postwar decades, replaced young adults as the main audience for most new forms of pop music. From the start, Rock and roll was party and dance music. It often celebrated the joys of being young, and it occasionally expressed the frustrations of youth – or "teenagers" as they were by then called – who generally rejected older styles of popular culture. Although rock and roll quickly became popular, its lyrics and the performance style that went with it were still considered indecent and outrageous by many adults, who either dismissed rock and roll as a passing trend or vehemently condemned it as a threat to good society. Most important for its young listeners, rock and roll was the first music that was all their own. Rock and roll proclaimed that being a teenager was special.

The economic boom that followed the end of WWII and the emergence of a youth culture helped rock and roll to displace the Tin Pan Alley songwriting tradition that had dominated the mainstream of North American pop taste since the late 1800s. Rock and roll music developed from a variety of different popular music styles. Its roots can be heard in the lyrics and electric guitar of the blues, combined with the jump blues R&B style, the doo-wop gospel-influenced vocal group style, the boogie-woogie or barrelhouse piano-blues style, and country music's honky-tonk and rockabilly styles. It was louder and faster than the forms from which it was inspired. Its texts contrasted sharply with the sentimental lyrics of earlier popular songs. And it was generally performed in a rowdy and spontaneous manner with a more primitive display of emotions.

Before rock and roll became a musical category, such R&B hits as 1951's *Rocket '88* by Jackie Brenston had the spirit of rock and roll. This and other similar records became increasingly popular with both black R&B and white country music audiences. Another forerunner of rock and roll was British "skiffle", a style of popular music in the 1950s that influenced the Beatles. Skiffle was based on American folk music and played on guitars and improvised percussion instruments.

Early on, the term rock and roll was actually a synonym for black R&B music. Rock and roll was first released by small, independent record companies like Sun Records and promoted by radio DJs like Alan Freed. To help attract white audiences unfamiliar with black R&B, Freed helped popularize the term rock and roll with his radio program, *Moondog Rock and Roll Party.*

The most successful rock and roll artists wrote and performed songs about a limited range of emotions and ideas including girls, boys, dances, love, sexuality, cars, identity crises, personal freedom, the joy of being young, and other issues that were of interest to teenagers. Bill Haley and the Comets, a country band from Pennsylvania that adopted aspects of the R&B jump blues style of Louis Jordan, became the first world famous rock act. Their recording of *Rock Around the Clock* in 1955 was the first international rock hit. It was used as the theme song for *The Blackboard Jungle*, a movie about juvenile delinquents. The song contributed to the rebellious reputation of rock and roll music.

Another rock and roll pioneer was blues musician Chuck Berry. Berry had been a hairdresser in St. Louis, Missouri, but found enormous success as a black singer and guitar player. His unique style came from his experience playing a mixture of blues, R&B, and country music in the American Midwest. He was the first of the legendary rock songwriters. His lyrics effectively expressed the feelings, issues, and problems of North American teenagers. Berry's first hit record, on Chicago's Chess label, was a 1955 country-styled song called *Maybellene*, which was quickly followed by the guitar driven classic *Johnny B. Goode.*

Other black rock and roll pioneers included Bo Diddley who unleashed an earthy style of guitar playing derived from the blues of the Mississippi Delta region. The rock and roll piano style of Louisiana musician Fats Domino grew out of the distinctive sound of New Orleans

R&B, while singer-songwriter Richard Penniman, known as Little Richard, was another advocate of this piano style. Little Richard helped influence rock performance styles with his vigorous, electrifying, and flamboyant stage performances. His first major success came in 1955 with *Tutti Frutti*.

The major rock and roll explosion began with singer Elvis Presley, the most significant early rock and roll artist. His arrival on the music scene can be likened to the "big bang" of modern popular music. Although he was white, he had the style commonly associated with increasingly popular black music. The popularity of his black sound combined with his exciting hip-shaking live performances and frequent radio play rapidly made Presley a superstar. His first major success came with his 1956 recording of *Heartbreak Hotel*, which was followed by many other hits and Hollywood films, transforming this Tennessee truck driver into the "King of Rock and Roll" and launching an amazing thirty year career.

Another young rock and roll innovator was Texan songwriter-guitarist Buddy Holly, who produced his own studio recordings and developed the standard four-piece instrumentation of rock bands. His numerous hits included *Peggy Sue* and *That'll be the Day*. Also during this period, singer-guitarist Ritchie Valens incorporated his Latin musical roots with the rock and roll beat and spirit to produce the hit song *La Bamba*, later covered by the American Latino band Los Lobos. Valens set the trend for rock music's long tradition of incorporating international influences.

The Everly Brothers were among the most important and best early rock and roll artists. Brothers Don and Phil set unmatched standards for close, two-part harmonies and infused early rock and roll with some of the best elements of country and popular music. Their legacy was and is felt in all rock performers that employ harmonies as significant features.

Radio played an important role in spreading rock and roll during the mid-1950s and contributed to its growing popularity. Television had replaced radio as the main producer of entertainment, and many radio stations began to play rock and roll music to capture an audience. DJs who played the records became powerful forces in promoting the popularity of rock and roll artists.

Though the United States was racially segregated, some folks sensed a spirit of racial equality in rock and roll. It featured black artists, who were influenced by white country music. It also presented white artists, who adopted styles based on black R&B. In earlier times, the recordings of such Southern black musicians would have been categorized as race records, and marketed to African American consumers. With the arrival of rock and roll, these musicians appealed to black and white audiences alike, as seen in the success of such black doo-wop singing groups as the Penguins, the Chords, and the Platters.

The appeal of rock and roll to white middle-class teenagers was immediate and caught the major record labels by surprise. As rock and roll continued to grow in popularity, the major record labels and professional composers who had ignored the music started to recognize rock and roll's profitability. By the late 1950s, much of what record labels released as rock and roll was no longer exciting, spontaneous, and rebellious. The golden age of rock and roll had passed. While rock continued to sell well, the music was much tamer than it had been just a few years earlier. As these companies moved to capitalize on the popularity of the style, the market was energized by mainstream cover versions of R&B songs that were edited for suggestive lyrics and performed in the vocal style known as crooning by white singers such as Pat Boone, Bobby Darin, and Frankie Avalon. They had toned down the volume and the feel of the music. As a result, the peak period of rock and roll was over. The genre experienced an artistic decline and became just another form of popular music.

Rock and roll also lost many of its stars and creative forces toward the end of the 1950s. In 1958, Elvis Presley was drafted into the United States Army and Jerry Lee Lewis caused a scandal by marrying his 13-year-old cousin. Then in 1959, Chuck Berry was arrested; Buddy Holly, Ritchie Valens, and rock and roll novelty act the Big Bopper died in an airplane crash; and, Little Richard left show business to study for the ministry.

By the early 1960s, the pop music industry was assembling professional composers, hired studio session musicians, and bland white teenage crooners such as Fabian, Bobby Rydell, Dion and Bobby Vinton, to mass-produce songs that imitated late-50s rock and roll. In the early 60s, New York songwriters such as Neil Sedaka and Carole King composed numerous hit songs, many of which were recorded by female vocal ensembles known as "girl groups", such as the Ronettes, the Chiffons, and the Shirelles. Also during this era, the role of the record producer was expanded by musical mastermind Phil Spector, a producer who created numerous hits by using elaborate studio techniques in a dense orchestral approach called the "wall of sound".

The early 1960s saw the development of distinctive regional styles in North America, such as the Detroit sound produced by the Motown record company. The young entrepreneur and record producer, Berry Gordy, utilized some of the writing techniques of Tin Pan Alley, particularly the idea of teaming professional lyricists with melody composers. Working this way, Gordy's Motown Records produced a bevy of hit songs throughout the 60s and expanded the market for music by African American artists purchased by white teenagers. Popular Motown crossover groups included the Supremes, the Temptations, the Four Tops, the Miracles, Martha & the Vandellas, and the Jackson 5 featuring Michael Jackson.

Other regional styles also developed during this epoch, such as the unvarnished sound of American Northwest bands the Sonics and the Kingsmen, who had one big hit *Louie, Louie* that defined the garage-band style. The New York-Greenwich Village and Washington Square urban folk movement included music by the Kingston Trio, Peter, Paul & Mary, Simon & Garfunkel, and the Mamas & the Papas featuring John Phillips. Phillips was the driving creative force behind their artistic and commercial success – writing the hits *Monday, Monday*, and *California Dreamin'*. And finally, Philadelphia showcased all styles on Dick Clark's American Bandstand television program.

Prolific singer and lyricist Bob Dylan epitomized the Greenwich Village movement. Dylan began his musical career in the early 1960s as a solo folk singer and follower of Woody Guthrie. His popularity began among many fans of early rock and roll that had dismissed the music of the early 60s as uninspired. They began listening to folk music for its social significance. Folk music fans turned to Dylan for his social conscience and protest songs. These songs protested what many people considered the wrongs and injustices of society, such as racial prejudice, poverty, lack of freedom, and war. The powerful social message of Dylan's songs influenced many young musicians.

The city of Nashville displayed its Tennessee brand of rock with the 1960 release of *Only the Lonely* by Roy Orbison. Orbison went on to record eight more chart toppers, including *Crying* in 1961 and *Oh, Pretty Woman* in 1964. Equally popular were the rich harmonic "surf" sound of the southern California bands. The Beach Boys became the most popular surf music group. They sang of surfing, hot rods, and teen dreams. They became famous for their fine vocal harmonies, as well as the experimental production techniques of the band's leading songwriter Brian Wilson.

In February 1964 the Beatles arrived in New York to appear on The Ed Sullivan Show television program and launched the so-called "British Invasion". Influenced by North American recordings, British popular groups of the period invigorated the pop music mainstream by returning the excitement to rock and roll, thereby confirming the international stature of rock music. The Beatles, a quartet from Liverpool, England, made rock music more popular than ever and more respected artistically. Their witty and sophisticated songs made the sentimental rock of the time appear tame, stale, and old-fashioned. The Beatles consisted of four lads in their early twenties, namely John Lennon, Paul McCartney, George Harrison, and Ringo Starr. Although celebrated in Britain since 1962, their American breakthrough came in 1964 with *I Want to Hold Your Hand*, written by Lennon and McCartney. They eventually established themselves as the most popular songwriting team in rock's history. The Beatles' first hit singles in North America were released through small, independent record companies, because major labels did not initially take the British groups seriously. Revered English record producer George Martin helped to shape the Fab Four's revolutionary studio sound.

Beatlemania was the term employed to describe the excitement generated by the band. Guided by their dedicated manager Brian Epstein, Beatlemania changed international pop culture. It affected North American society in numerous ways, including hairstyle, fashion and merchandizing. Teen-age girls screamed so loudly during the group's performances that it was impossible to hear the music. Initially, many parents feared the effects of Beatlemania. But the personal charm and musical appeal of the group quickly conquered older audiences as well. The Beatles turned rock and roll from an American-dominated musical style into an international phenomenon by combining the guitar-based rock and roll of Chuck Berry and Buddy Holly with the craftwork of Tin Pan Alley composers. Soon after the Beatles hit the United States, British groups that wrote and played their own music filled the pop music charts. The British bands replaced American solo singers who relied primarily on outside songwriters and musicians.

Soon, several British Invasion bands had developed iconoclastic styles. For example, the Animals combined blues and R&B influences and produced a hit in 1964 with an old Anglo-American ballad, *House of the Rising Sun*. The Rolling Stones, featuring innovative guitarist Keith Richards and charismatic singer Mick Jagger, blended aspects of Chicago blues to their distinctive, forceful sound. The Stones were the most significant of the bands that followed the Beatles to North America. They represented a dangerous and more rebellious alternative to the bouncy Merseybeat of the Beatles. Their gritty, hard-driving style was more faithful to its roots in the blues. The Stones pioneered the blues-based rock and roll that came to define hard rock. Other British bands that joined the Invasion forces included Herman's Hermits, The Who, the Kinks, Gerry & the Pacemakers, and the Dave Clark Five, who initially seemed the biggest challenger to the Beatles' phenomenon with their 1964 hit *Glad All Over*.

The incredible success of the British groups caused some North America artists to change or develop their own styles. In 1965 Bob Dylan helped swing the balance of popularity away from the British and back to North American musicians. Following the example of the Beatles, Dylan began playing his material live and in-studio on electric guitar with a band that used electrically amplified instruments; alienating many folk-music purists in the process. Dylan's new electric style was vehemently denounced with jeers during his performance at the 1965 Newport Folk Festival. Gradually, Dylan's songs became less political and more poetic and personal. He had one of his first and biggest rock hits in 1965 with *Like a Rolling Stone*. Dylan's ambitious, poetic lyrics set to a rock beat produced a style known as folk rock. The folk rock style was further pioneered by the American band the Byrds, who had a number-one hit on the music charts with a rendition of Dylan's song *Mr. Tambourine Man*. Folk rock was the first major challenge to rock's domination by the British.

By the mid-1960s rock and roll had earned wide respect as a legitimate art form. The music's popularity spread worldwide among listeners of all ages. By the end of the 60s, the music had moved far from its roots in blues and country, and it became known simply as rock. Rock's signature characteristics however, remained faithful to a driving backbeat, raw emotional vocals, and wailing amplified guitars.

The mid-1960s became a time of incredible creativity for rock music. Rock artists explored new possibilities in lyrical content and form. Some began to examine the meaning of dreams in their lyrics. Others began to use free-verse poetry that did not rhyme. The Beatles'

1967 album *Sgt. Pepper's Lonely Hearts Club Band* established new standards for studio recording, and helped to establish the notion of the rock musician as a creative artist. The album was a masterpiece consisting of innovative studio experiments producing a succession of musical pieces linked together by a loose narrative theme or story line, making it the first rock "concept album". Once again, North American musicians responded to the British musical innovations by experimenting with new forms, technologies, and stylistic influences.

San Francisco rock, or psychedelic rock, emerged about 1966 and was closely associated with the use of hallucinogenic drugs, such as LSD (Lysergic Acid Diethylamide) or "acid," and an emphasis on spontaneity and communitarian values, epitomized in free-form events called "be-ins". This so-called "free love" generation produced psychedelic art and light shows. Artists such as Jerry Garcia and the Grateful Dead experimented with long, improvised stretches of music called "jams". Despite the antiestablishment stance of the youth culture in the "city by the bay", San Francisco psychedelia attracted attention from the important recording companies, offering lucrative contracts to such artists as Jefferson Airplane, Janis Joplin, and Santana featuring guitar wiz Carlos Santana.

Another important focal point of rock music in the late 1960s was Los Angeles, where film student Jim Morrison formed the band the Doors and guitarist-composer Frank Zappa developed an idiosyncratic style of complex jazz-influenced compositional forms with his band the Mothers of Invention. Creedence Clearwater Revival also joined the fray led by songwriter, guitarist John Fogerty.

In the late 60s "hard rock" emerged, focusing on thick layers of sound, loud volume levels, and skillful guitar solos. In London, American guitar hero Jimi Hendrix developed a highly influential electric guitar style. His fiery guitar virtuosity extended the range of the instrument by manipulating its switches and pedals to create new sounds. In 1966 the first so-called "power trio" was formed in London, England. The group Cream showcased the technical brilliance of guitarist Eric Clapton, bassist Jack Bruce, and drummer Ginger Baker. Instrumentalists such as Hendrix and Clapton began exercising more creative freedom by stretching a single song to about ten or twenty minutes. Blues and jazz traditions inspired their extended solos. The music played by such groups as the Jimi Hendrix Experience and Clapton's Cream were sometimes categorized as progressive rock.

Some of their music was also called acid rock, after the illegal drug that was growing in popularity among some rock fans.

During this period additional rock styles emerged in North America. "Southern rock" was pioneered by the Allman Brothers Band, "jazz-rock" was introduced by the band Blood, Sweat and Tears, and "Latin rock" – a blend of Latin American music, jazz and rock influences, and R&B styles – was showcased by the music of Santana.

The growing influence and popularity of rock music continued to affect society in a number of ways. Some rock music encouraged the use of illicit drugs. Other rock music inspired public protest against such social and political problems as racial prejudice and the Vietnam War. In addition, rock was featured in many popular theatre works, including the 1967 stage production of *Hair*.

Toward the end of the 1960's, rock's various styles came together at large-scale outdoor rock festivals. These festivals showed how popular and diverse the music had become. The most significant rock festivals were San Francisco's *Monterey International Pop Music Festival* during 1967's "summer of love", followed by the 1969 *Woodstock Music and Arts Festival* in upstate New York. Woodstock was a musical, communal celebration of the alternative "hippie" culture and lifestyle, dedicated to "peace and love". The event drew more than 300,000 fans and featured three days of top rock performers such as the powerhouse blues singer Janis Joplin, who first gained massive exposure at these rock festivals.

As the 1970s began, rock music diversified further into new styles and complex forms while consolidating its position in the mainstream of North American pop music. A new youth-oriented popular market was defined by a broad category of rock music, which now included Southern rock, hard rock, jazz-rock, country rock, folk rock, blues-rock, and other styles.

Rock reached its economic zenith in the early 1970s, as it became a bigger business than ever. It not only dominated the music industry, but also influenced everything from fashion to film to politics. These years were also a time of corporate expansion and stylistic diversification in the North American record industry. Although the early 70s found rock more profitable than ever, in terms of musical quality, some considered the period rocks lowest point since the early 60s. As a widening audience increasingly accepted rock, many complained it had lost much of the youthful vigor and spirit of rebellion that had originally powered it. By the mid-70s, the music started to reclaim some of the inspiration and intensity associated with earlier rock. The working-class bar-band hero Bruce Springsteen and the E Street Band attracted an enthusiastic following in 1975 with the album *Born to Run*. Springsteen's music reflected the energetic rock and roll and R&B music of the 1950s. He demonstrated with aplomb how rock might carve out a future by delving into its heritage.

Throughout the 1970s, almost every pop music style contained elements of rock. The music's audience spanned from preteens to middle-aged adults. As the audience for rock expanded, a variety of new musical categories developed. The decade's popular mainstream was dominated by superstar rock bands, such as the Rolling Stones, Fleetwood Mac, Chicago, the Doobie Brothers, the Eagles, Paul McCartney and Wings, and by individual superstars, such as Elton John, Billy Joel, Rod Stewart, and Stevie Wonder. Each of these acts produced million selling albums pushing the industry to operate at a new grander scale. Also fashionable was the singer-songwriter genre, an outgrowth of urban, acoustic folk music led by James Taylor, Carole King, Jackson Browne, Canadian Joni Mitchell, and others who popularized this style by composing music with thoughtful, often autobiographical, lyrics. Popular as well in the 70s was a widely listened to light pop-rock style called "adult contemporary", exemplified by radio friendly mainstream artists such as Barry Manilow, Dionne Warwick, Neil Diamond, Tom Jones, Englebert Humperdink, and Barbra Streisand.

At the other end of the stylistic spectrum, bands Deep Purple, Led Zeppelin, and Black Sabbath featuring Ozzy Osbourne, all of which stressed screaming electric guitars in their songs, pioneered the aggressive "heavy-metal" style. Musical groups such as Roxy Music, King Crimson, Yes, Emerson, Lake and Palmer, Gentle Giant and Genesis, combined a rock beat with the more complex melodies of classical music and displays of technical skill with spectacular stage shows, creating the "Art rock" style. "Glitter rock", or "glam rock", cultivated a decadent image exemplified by the band Kiss and solo musicians Alice Cooper, David Bowie, Marc Bolan, and the early career of Lou Reed. These acts popularized flamboyant theatrical onstage visuals by wearing heavy makeup and sequined costumes and sometimes presenting themselves as sexually androgynous.

The early 70s witnessed the development of "funk", a variant of soul music that was influenced by rock. Influential funk artists included the San Francisco group Sly and the Family Stone, and singer George Clinton, whose bands Parliament and Funkadelic intermingled science-fiction imagery and social satire with jazz-influenced horn music, long improvised jams, vocal group harmonies, and African-derived rhythms.

The most popular dance music of the 70s was "disco". Initially associated with the gay subculture of Manhattan, disco drew upon African American pop music and simplified rhythms by adding steady bass-drum beats. Although much despised by hard rock fans, disco had a substantial impact on rock music, especially after the release of the 1977 movie *Saturday Night Fever* and its incredibly successful disco soundtrack, featuring the Bee Gees. Disco often combined Latin rhythms, a type of earthy blues, and elements of funk to produce a strong, steady dance beat. It was created primarily for dance clubs called discotheques, or discos. It was rarely performed live. Instead, discos played tapes and records of the music. Popular disco artists included "Disco Queen" Donna Summer, the Village People, Abba, and Chic – arguably disco's greatest band. Although many people considered disco to be mindless formula music, disco returned dancing and the spirit of fun to pop music. At a time when many white rock radio stations were giving little exposure to African American artists, disco appealed to a diverse audience with dance music recorded by both black and white acts.

The mid-70s saw the appearance of "punk rock" and "new wave" music, originating in London and New York City. This movement arouse partly as a backlash against the technical, impersonal sounds of disco, but also as a reaction against the lack of inspiration and commercialism of mainstream rock, and the pretentiousness of art rock. Inspired by antiestablishment icon Iggy Pop, punk rock attempted to launch a rock revolution with its crude, abrasive, and fast sound. British punk bands included the Clash, the Sex Pistols, and the Police featuring Sting. New York punk music was introduced by the Stooges and the New York Dolls, but fully realized by the Ramones. Such bands as Talking Heads and the Patti Smith Group took an artier approach to punk rock. Their music was more poetic and conceptually original than punk. These bands became categorized as punk's new wave of rock. Punk rock artists returned to the raw and unvarnished energy of earlier rock. They were fueled by anger at the materialism of society. The music of punk and new wave groups represented an aggressive and fresh alternative to the more established artists who dominated the rock world. Punk was not a big commercial success, but it had several important effects on rock music. It showed that new styles could develop outside the established rock industry. It also proved that young artists could express themselves without expensive equipment and years of training. Punk rock influenced many non-punk artists to make their music simpler, faster, and more energetic.

Initially, disco and punk were considered opposites. But they came together in the late seventies. The B-52's, the Buggles, The Go-Go's, Blondie and other bands enjoyed hits that combined disco rhythms with the spirit of new wave rock. With their sleek, mechanical new wave-pop-rock, The Cars racked up a string of platinum albums and Top 40 singles that made them one of the most popular North American bands of the late '70s and early '80s.

Also in the mid-1970s, "reggae" music, developed by artists in the shantytowns of the capitol city of Jamaica, Kingston began to attract attention among listeners in North America and the United Kingdom. The style, associated with political protest and the Rastafarian religion, combined elements of Jamaican folk music with R&B influences. The 1973 motion picture *The Harder They Come*, which starred reggae singer Jimmy Cliff in the role of an underclass gangster, stimulated reggae's popularity among North American university students. The superstar of the style was singer Bob Marley. The reggae music of Marley and his band the Wailers injected fresh inspiration into the sounds of the mid-70s with its slow, pulsing rhythms and smooth, soulful singing. By the time of Marley's death in 1981, he had become one of the most popular artists in the world. Anticipated by reggae, worldbeat music began to emerge during the late 70s and eventually reaffirmed the worldwide appeal of rock music.

During the 1970s the music industry in North America consolidated its power and became more centralized. Slick album productions and superstars groups played to massive crowds in sports arenas. These so-called "corporate rock" bands – represented by Styx, Supertramp, Queen, Boston, Reo Speedwagon, Foreigner, Cheap Trick, April Wine, and Journey – helped define a new pop mainstream. Spontaneous Woodstock-type mass gatherings had been replaced by carefully managed stadium concerts. The individualistic local radio programming of the late 60s was substituted with national radio formatting, in which music customized to sell products to target audiences was distributed nationally on tape to be broadcast from local stations. Economic factors prompted major record labels to pursue almost exclusively acts with the potential to sell millions of albums. While profits from hit albums had risen significantly, the financial risks involved in producing such music had also greatly increased. For five years, from 1978 to 1982, the North American rock-music industry experienced financial hardships as record sales fell drastically and income from live gigs experienced a similar precipitous decline. The industry became cautious due to this alarming drop in business.

A number of key factors contributed to an economic resurgence in the music industry during the mid-1980s. The advent of the music video and the debut in 1981 of MTV – a 24-hour music video television network – helped revive record sales. MTV and its clones became a new means for promoting songs and artists. In addition to music, these short films included acting, dancing, striking visual images, and sometimes excerpts from rock concert performances. Rock videos were shown on commercial and cable TV and at many dance clubs. Many songs became as popular for the visual element of the video as they did for the music. Some pop artists, such as Duran Duran, Culture Club, George Michael, Cyndi Lauper, and the Eurythmics, owe much of their success to the widespread exposure and massive popularity of their videos. The introduction of the digitally recorded compact disc or "CD" in 1983 also stimulated demand for pop music. Cassette tapes and CDs eventually overtook phonograph records as the most popular media for sound recording in the late 80s.

The 1982 album *Thriller* by American singer, dancer, and entertainer Michael Jackson became the biggest-selling record in history up to that time, and brought dormant music buyers back into the retail record stores. It established a pattern by which record companies relied upon a few massive hits to generate profits. Jackson's success also contributed to proving the promotional value of music videos. He starred in several highly innovative videos and became one of the most popular performers in the history of rock music. It thereafter became difficult for record labels to achieve hit records without intensive airplay on music-video channels.

The other mainstream pop-rock hits of the 1980s came from a new set of charismatic personalities, each of whom appealed to mass crossover audiences. Singer-songwriter Lionel Ritchie, former group leader of the Commodores, scored multiple consecutive international hits. Prince, whose 1984 single *When Doves Cry*, from his brilliant film soundtrack album *Purple Rain*, was the first song in more than two decades to top both the mainstream pop music charts and R&B charts. Singer Madonna marketed herself as a pop icon and came to symbolize female sexual liberation through her controversial videos, images, and lyrics. Bruce Springsteen's impressive artistic and commercial success, begun in the mid-1970s, carried over into the next decade.

Also during the 80s the audience for hard rock and heavy metal expanded from its original white-male, working-class core to include more middle-class fans, both male and female. By the end of the decade, bands such as AC/DC, Van Halen, Bon Jovi, Def Leppard, and Metallica, accounted for as much as forty percent of all records sold in North America. Offshoots of the heavy metal style were the so-call hard rock "hair bands". They sometimes gave the impression that they focused more on the styling of their coiffures than the originality of their music. Notwithstanding, the best bands of this genre such as Mötley Crüe, Poison, and White Snake, attained notable success.

Music from the 1960s inspired some of rock's most popular artists of the 1980's. Among these was the American group R.E.M., which drew heavily from 60s folk rock. In addition, many musicians who had begun their careers in the 60s achieved greater popularity than ever before. Some acts from the sixties, such as Tina Turner, the Who, the Rolling Stones, the Grateful Dead, and Pink Floyd, were among the leading concert attractions of the 80s. These artists remained popular not only with their original audience from the 60s but with new and younger fans as well.

During the 1980s, rock extended its importance as a catalyst for social change through a broadening interest in international issues and a reawakening of its social idealism. Rock's conscience and internationalism came together in such events as Live Aid, an all-day concert held in the summer of 1985. Money raised by the event went to help feed starving people in Ethiopia. The concert, held in both Philadelphia and London, was televised throughout the world and featured many of the biggest stars in rock, including musician Phil Collins who boarded the Concord jet in order to perform in both cities.

Various rock artists, including the heavy metal bands Twisted Sister and Guns n' Roses, sparked controversy with their rebellious lyrics, aggressive music, and antisocial positions. Concerned parents, led by Tipper Gore, and such organizations as the Parents' Music Resource Center successfully called for record companies to attach warning labels to albums with lyrics that might be improper or objectionable. Cynics of this policy later pointed out that these warning labels actually helped increase sales.

Since 1980, rock has continued to reflect an ongoing technological revolution. Computers and synthesizers have often replaced guitars and drums. Rhythm machines, synthesizers, and computers have also been extensively used with dance and rap music. Perhaps the most significant rock-music development of the 80s was the rise of rap, a genre in which vocalists perform rhythmic speech, usually accompanied by music samples from prerecorded material or from music created by synthesizers. Electronic music or "techno" is a style of dance music developed in the 80s that combines computer-generated, disco-like rhythms with digital samples. Played on electronic instruments and created with extensive use of studio technology, techno produces a futuristic, machine-made sound. Depeche Mode was the quintessential electro-pop band of the 80s. These instruments have influenced the recording of more traditional rock as well. Even for concert performances, musicians have mixed live music with preprogrammed computer and synthesizer backing. As a result, it has become difficult to distinguish "live" music from taped or "canned," music. In 1990, the dance-oriented duo Milli Vanilli was stripped of its Grammy award for "best new artist" when they revealed that they had not actually sung on their recordings, but had simply mouthed or "lip-synced" vocals recorded by others.

Rock music in the 1990s matured and expanded to include hundreds of musical styles, some of which define a broad mainstream, while others were supported by small but devoted audiences. As in earlier decades, major record companies have relied on independent labels to discover new trends and find promising talent. "Techno" music gained wide popularity in the 90s at all-night dance parties called "raves". Heavy metal remained popular, as evidenced by massive arena and stadium concerts featuring such groups as Judas Priest, Slayer and Megadeth. A style known as "alternative rock", popularized in the late 1980s by R.E.M., combines heavy-metal guitars, folk and punk influences, and dark, introspective lyrics. The alternative style generated various sub styles, such as the grunge rock of Seattle-based bands Soundgarden, Pearl Jam, and Nirvana featuring Kurt Cobain.

Rap and heavy metal moved closer to the mainstream of rock culture in the early 1990s. At the same time, rock musicians continued to explore international music as a source of inspiration. The decade also witnessed the popular supremacy of dance pop artists who appealed to a younger audience, as rock grew older. Superstars Paula Abdul,

Kylie Minogue, and Janet Jackson dominated the charts and were later succeeded by Britney Spears, Justin Timberlake and Christina Aguilera. The lucrative youth market was also increasingly captivated by the "boy-band" style, a phenomenon started in the eighties by the New Kids On The Block and more recently continued by groups like Backstreet Boys and NSYNC. Latin American pop music also flourished with the popularity of superstar artists Gloria Estefan, Ricky Martin, Shakira, Jennifer Lopez, and Marc Anthony.

As rock music broadened and expanded during its first four decades, rock itself increasingly became an object of nostalgia. In 1995 the Rock and Roll Hall of Fame opened in Cleveland, Ohio. Also in the 1990s and early 2000s, several television documentaries and films were produced on the history of rock and roll, and historical CD & DVD box-set recordings were reissued featuring pioneering artists.

Since its inception in the mid-1950s, rock has been shaped by a multifaceted relationship between the symbolic freedom of the rebellious rock artist, and big-business control. Originally a mixture of styles outside the mainstream of white middle-class popular taste, rock and roll soon became a mass-produced commodity. This conflict between individuality and commercialism remains a concern in rock music and is reflected in fan disdain for artists who compromise, or "sell out", their musical principles in order to obtain lucrative recording contracts. Shaped by the growth of the mass media, technology, and the social identities of its musicians and fans, rock continues to play a pivotal role in North America's pop culture and, increasingly, the world.

From its origins, rock has moved from the margins of North American pop music to become the center of a global industry. Closely connected with youth culture, rock music and musicians have helped to establish new trends in fashion, language, political views, and social priorities. However, rock is no longer limited to an audience of teenagers, since many current fans formed their musical tastes during the golden age of rock and roll. Similarly, while rock has historically fueled new creative expressions, the innovations of pioneering musicians have defined a tradition to which successive generations of artists have repeatedly turned for inspiration.

Since its creation, rock music has continued to defy musical barriers and has drawn much of its strength from international musical influences. At present, rock music is no longer only the music of young North Americans. It is music of the world.

Harry Belafonte

Ravi Shankar

Bob Marley

Paul Simon

Peter Gabriel

8. WORLDBEAT

In the Western world, "world music" refers either to music that doesn't fall into the British and North American folk or pop traditions or to hybrids of various indigenous types of music. Certain styles, such as Latin pop or Jamaican reggae grew large enough to be classified as their own genre, but everything else, from African folk to traditional Chinese music, is classified as world music. "Worldbeat" is something different than world music, since it's usually the result of Western fusions and hybrids, yet it still falls under the world music umbrella because it borrows sounds, instrumentation, and styles from various indigenous kinds of music.

The term worldbeat refers not to one specific genre of music, but to a certain sensibility – namely, the fusion of dissimilar musical idioms in ways that are only possible from a global, multicultural perspective. The results can range from Westernized dance or pop music to wild, style-fusing experimentalism, but the main, unifying characteristic of worldbeat is its conscious attempt to bring world music to a broader audience. At its best, worldbeat can produce amazing eclecticism and unique hybrids.

Worldbeat is a term that represents various styles of world pop music that are practiced outside the European-North American mainstream. The term is used by the Western music industry to group a variety of non-Western forms of pop music including the rhythms of Third World countries. Worldbeat also connotes world pop music that has been influenced by Western pop, or, conversely, Western pop music that incorporates non-Western traditional folk, art, or ethnic musical influences such as African music; Arab music; Chinese music; Greek music; Indian music; Indonesian music; Latin American music and African American music. There is also a rich history of syncretism or cross-fertilization between popular styles. For example, in the late 1800s the Cuban habanera influenced the development of American ragtime; the Argentine tango gained global popularity during the 1910s, initiating a worldwide craze for Latin ballroom dancing; recordings of country music, Hawaiian guitar music, and ballroom dance bands arrived in the port cities of Africa by the 1920s; and the Cuban rumba became popular internationally in the 30s.

As popular music first emerged in the early twentieth century, numerous pop music styles also began to develop around the globe. The rise of such genres was linked to dramatic transformations occurring throughout the world. For example, urbanization and modernization disrupted traditional attitudes, lifestyles, and forms of artistic patronage, while creating new urban social classes with new musical and cultural tastes. In addition, the emerging pop music styles were closely tied to the infiltration of mass media. The spread of recording technology in the 1920s and 30s introduced new forms of mass production and broadcasting of both local and imported music. Many of the new evolving pop music styles consisted of hybrids that combined native folk traditions with modern stylistic qualities drawn from abroad. Urban-centered, mass-reproduced pop music outside of Western culture was active in Asia, Africa, and Latin America, and local pop styles were commercially recorded by the 1920s.

In many non-Western societies, the emerging pop music styles bridged Western imports, such as the piano, guitar and chordal harmony, with traditional qualities, such as indigenous musical form, and trademark melody, rhythm, and singing style. In large societies, the cultural mixes could be more complex. For example, Cuban dance musicians blended elements of Spanish-derived folk music with influences from American jazz, developing styles such as the "mambo", a fast dance genre for big band, and the "bolero", a slow, sentimental song style. These Cuban dance-music forms became popular around the world.

Anticipated by reggae in the 1970s, "ethno pop" began to emerge during the early 80s, with the success of the 1982 album *Juju Music* by Nigerian musician King Sunny Ade. Ade's music, which combined traditional African drums with electric guitars and synthesizers, helped to stimulate an interest in non-Western music in Great Britain and North America, and opened the way for musicians as diverse as the Gipsy Kings, from France; Ladysmith Black Mombazo, from South Africa; Papa Wemba, from Congo; Ofra Haza, from Israel; and Nusrat Fateh Ali Khan, from Pakistan.

While the term worldbeat was not commonly used until the 1980s, non-Western styles of music had been introduced in Europe much earlier. Classical composer Mozart imitated Turkish military music in his famous 1778 *Turkish March*, and French composer Georges Bizet used a popular nineteenth-century Cuban dance form and tune or "habanera" in his 1875 opera *Carmen*. With the arrival of records, several non-Western music genres enjoyed popularity in North America and Europe from the 1920s. Hawaiian music was perhaps the single most popular style of commercial music in North America in the 20s. During the 40s and 50s the North America experienced the so-called mambo craze, the chachachá fad, and the successful marketing of Trinidadian calypso by American vocalist Harry Belafonte. In the early 60s a few records that derived from distinct ethnic origins achieved places on the pop charts, including a 1959 rock and roll recording of the Mexican folk song *La Bamba*, performed by rocker Ritchie Valens. Other hits included the 1964 "ska", a fast style of dance music song, version of *My Boy Lollipop* performed by Jamaican singer Millie Small, and *Pata Pata* of 1967, written and performed by South African vocalist Miriam Makeba. Several Beatles songs attained international popularity as a direct result of the musical influence of Indian sitarist Ravi Shankar. Brazilian bossa novas became commercial hits as well as jazz standards, including 1964's *The Girl from Ipanema* by Brazilian songwriter Antonio Carlos Jobim.

It was not until the 1970s, however, that music genres from outside the Western mainstream came to be appreciated as more than fads or novelty sounds. In particular, Jamaican reggae achieved international popularity. Reggae, whose antecedent, ska, developed partly as a Jamaican reinterpretation of American R&B music, became popular not only for its gripping rhythms and its soulful melodies, but also for its inspiring ideology. Expressed via the Afro-centric principles of the West Indian Rastafarian religion, reggae's fervent and utopian message of peace, justice, idealism, and liberation, had international appeal. As rock-audiences listened to Bob Marley's music, and as musicians such as English rock guitarist Eric Clapton recorded reggae songs, a fresh dimension of internationalism and multiculturalism entered the international music industry.

The 1980s witnessed the development of a global awareness and fragmentation of pop music into myriad forms and syncretic approaches. The rise of worldbeat confirmed the new worldwide popularity of non-Western genres of popular music. Although the rock world was never closed to outside influence, the Western audience for world music really started to take shape when rock artists began to incorporate ethnic sounds into their recordings, and pursued high-profile collaborations with world-music artists. With the commercial possibilities presented by a greatly expanded potential audience, some artists began to tailor their music for international appeal.

One of the major developments in pop music in the late 1980s and early 90s was the emergence of "ethno beat", a broad category of worldbeat that includes such diverse musical styles as Canada's Northern Inuit throat singing, Yemenite Israeli dance music, Bulgarian women's choral music, Japanese salsa bands, Caribbean rhythms, and African dance styles. A landmark in the latter trend was the 1988 award-winning album *Graceland*, by American musician Paul Simon, which represented a widely successful collaboration between Simon and black South African musicians. *Graceland* played an important role in exposing ethno beat to audiences in Europe and North America.

Four years later, Simon delivered *The Rhythm of the Saints*, which did for Brazilian music what *Graceland* had done for South African music and was another multi-platinum seller. Simon, along with vocalist David Byrne of Talking Heads, British rock superstar Peter Gabriel, musician Mickey Hart, and others went on to produce eclectic recordings in collaboration with Chicano, Brazilian, West African, and "Newyorican" or New York City Puerto Rican musicians, among others. In working with instrumentalists outside the Euro-American mainstream, these artists appear to have been inspired by an interest in fresh sounds as well as by a search for music that seemed authentic and uncontaminated by the commercial music industry. Some have criticized these Western artists of exploiting musicians from developing countries, for uprooting traditional styles and diluting them for mass consumption. Others, however, have praised their efforts to promote and popularize their non-Western collaborators.

Although there were many exceptions, the majority of the worldbeat musicians who achieved a degree of popularity in the West came from Africa, a continent whose music had already exerted a tremendous influence on Western pop music throughout the twentieth century. Thus, the sounds of artists like Salif Keita from Mali, Mory Kante from Guinea, and Youssou N'Dour from Senegal were familiar enough to be appealing, yet different enough to be striking and intriguing. Other worldbeat artists use their broad range of musical knowledge to find similarities and common ground among different indigenous traditions from around the world. Musician Johnny Clegg brought the South African white and black musical cultures together. The music of Clegg and his Zulu dance group Savuka was well received by North American audiences and reached its peak with the 1993 album, *Heat, Dust And Dreams*, which was nominated for a Grammy in the "best world music" category and received a Billboard music award as "Best World Music Album".

While language is often a barrier to the cross-cultural popularity of certain types of music, styles of worldbeat dance music have gained success in the West. Although African and Caribbean popular music form the core of worldbeat, a few other styles have merited international popularity. More North Americans now explore with curiosity and enthusiasm new releases of everything from Egyptian Arabic music, Nigerian "juju", South African "isicathamiya", and Tibetan chant, to tribal songs and ambient sounds from the jungles of New Guinea. Other styles include Sufi devotional music, Sundanese gong-chime ensembles or "jaipongan", and Vietnamese theater-derived music or "vong co". Audiophiles often enjoy not only modernist eclectic recordings, but also purely indigenous traditional music such as the Zulu choral singing style of South Africa, Greek "rebetika", and central African Congolese "soukous" – a blend of indigenous songs and dance rhythms with Afro-Cuban music. The rich variety of pop music found around the globe continually feeds the international music industry with fresh music trends.

Worldbeat has never been a commercial juggernaut in the West, but some of the better-known genres include the popular music of West Africa and South Africa, North African "rai" from Algeria, Bulgarian choral music, Tuvan throat singing, Scandinavian folk, various forms of Indian music (raga, dance, and film music), Pakistani qawwali, Brazilian samba, Spanish flamenco, and Argentinian tango, to name just a few that have made an impact among open-minded critics and adventurous record buyers.

One recent example of a new popular global trend can be heard in "new age" music. Born from an aesthetic that aims to induce a sense of inner calm, new age music emerged from the meditational and holistic fields. Generally, these are harmonious and non-threatening albums that are allied with new age philosophies encouraging spiritual transcendence and physical healing. Some of these records are artistically fulfilling as well as therapeutic. Lesser musicians, however, often make dubious claims as to their ability to transport listeners into advanced spiritual states through specially designed sonic vibrations and perfectly conceived musical ideas. The main types of new age music are solo instrumental, progressive electronic, neo-classical, meditation, ethnic fusion, and contemporary instrumental. Some renowned artists include Steven Halpern, Mike Oldfield, Enya, Yanni, and Canadian instrumentalist Liona Boyd.

Easy Listening music is another style often tinged with world music influences. Easy Listening is instrumental music that was designed to be soothing and relaxing. Unlike jazz, which demands your undivided attention, easy listening slips into the background, which is the reason many people dismissed the music as disposable fluff. Although some recordings certainly fall into that category, there were many inventive arrangers and conductors working in the genre who distinguished themselves with unpredictable instrumentation and idiosyncratic arrangements. Still, the primary trademark of easy listening is that it's pleasant and easy on the ears. Well-known artists include Henry Mancini, Lawrence Welk, Herb Alpert, Ray Conniff, Martin Denny, Les Baxter, Esquivel, and Sergio Mendes.

In many cases, the exposure of Euro-American audiences to worldbeat music has been facilitated not only by the availability of recordings, but also by the abundance of immigrant communities in major cities. Some big-city nightclubs that hire worldbeat artists attract immigrants as well as Western world-music lovers. The presence of large numbers of Caribbean and African immigrants in large Western urban centers has helped make these cities focal points for world pop music. For example, New York has been the de facto center of the Latin-music industry since the 1940s; Paris is home to the top French Caribbean popular bands; and London's second-generation immigrants are developing their own hybrid styles, such as the *"bhangra"* music of British-born South Asians, which fuses "Punjabi" folk melodies and rhythms with influences from disco and modern Jamaican reggae.

The increasing homogenization and Westernization of the world's music is viewed in certain circles with apprehension. In many developing nations, the trend toward Westernization of their indigenous music continues unabated, greatly caused by the proliferation of the mass media by Western culture. In many cases, innovative crossover musicians, that syncretize two or more styles, are inspired by their exposure to Western music and by the changing tastes and demands of their urban audiences. At the same time, these artists sometimes seek to earn fame and fortune in the West. As a result, artists often try to craft sounds that appeal to Westerners while still retaining some unique indigenous flavor.

Although it is tempting to mourn what has been lost, the world musical community should nevertheless continue to celebrate what has been gained through this process – an exciting view and taste of the world's rich, diverse, and compelling music.

clockwise from top left: Run-DMC,
Public Enemy, Tupac Shakur, Jay Z

Eminem

9. RAP

The most important recent development in popular music has been the rise of rap, which originated as a genre of folk music growing out of black youth street culture in the South Bronx community of New York City in the mid-1970s. Rap music is a combination of rhymed words spoken over rhythm tracks and pieces of recorded music and sounds called samples, taken from older recordings. It was developed by black American urban disc jockeys, which began manipulating the vinyl records they were playing in dance clubs to make scratching rhythms and other sounds, creating a musical montage. A rapper would speak over the music, in street-language rhymes and vernacular that boasted of verbal or sexual prowess. Break dancing, including acrobatics, would often accompany the music.

A rap group consists of at least one rapper and a DJ, but two or more rappers are common. In groups with two, the rappers generally serve as foils for one another, alternating or completing lines and verses in a seamless pattern. The rap often uses a call-and-response format typical of much black American music.

The main inspiration for rap came from DJs in Jamaica, who would talk, or "toast", over recorded music they played in nightclubs. The style, known as "dub", produced pop records that featured disc jockeys talking over instrumental backing and electronic effects. The wordplay in a rap is rooted in African and black American verbal games of the late 1960s and 70s, known as "the dozens" and "signifying". The roots of rap music also lie in the poetry of several African American writers of the 1960s, such as the Watts Prophets and the Last Poets.

The Jamaican dub and toasting styles – joking, boasting, and using myriad in-group references – were taken to the Bronx by Jamaican immigrants and eventually were blended with new technologies, such as synthesizers and electronic drum machines. These topical streetwise rhymes and chants were often layered over "samples" of earlier artists to form new tunes. Samples consist of digitally isolated sound bites of existing musical recordings, often owned by another party. This particular use of samples and declaimed vocal styles became widespread in the pop music of both black and white performers. In the late-1980s, rap redefined, tested, and challenged established notions and concepts of musical composition, instruments, copyright protection, and intellectual property.

Sampling brought into question the ownership of sound. Some musicians claimed that by sampling recordings of a respected black performer such as funk artist James Brown, they were issuing an indirect challenge to the white corporate recording industry's right to own black cultural expression. More serious was the fact that rap musicians were also challenging Brown's and other artists' right to own, control, and be compensated for the use of their copyrighted intellectual property. By the early 1990s a system had come about whereby most musicians requested permission and negotiated some form of compensation for the use of samples. Some sampled artists, such as funk musician George Clinton, released CDs containing sound bites specifically to facilitate sampling. One effect of sampling was an awakening to musical history among black youth. Earlier musicians such as Brown and Clinton were fêted as cultural heroes and their older recordings were reissued and re-popularized.

Rap originated as a cross-cultural product. Most of its key early practitioners were recent Americans of Caribbean ancestry. In the early 1970s, a Jamaican deejay known as Kool DJ Herc moved to the Bronx and introduced the musical innovations that eventually developed into rap. Herc is the originator of breakbeat Djing. He was the first disc jockey to buy two copies of the same record for just a brief rhythmic instrumental segment or "break" in the middle. Using two turntables, Herc manipulated vinyl records by switching rapidly from one to the other to mix and match beats between two songs in a technique known as "cutting". He also developed "back-spinning", or rotating the disc by hand in order to repeat particular phrases. This created a collage of longer dance segments, over which, comments were shouted out to the dancers during the instrumental breaks. While he was cutting with two turntables, Herc would also perform with the microphone in Jamaican toasting style. Herc's musical parties gained notoriety and were often recorded on cassette tapes with the new boom box, or blaster, technology. Taped duplicates of these parties quickly made their way through the New York City boroughs, producing similar DJ acts.

Among the new breed of disc jockeys was Afrika Bambaataa, the first important Black Muslim in rap and considered by many to be the "godfather" of rap. Bambaataa often engaged in sound-system contests with Herc, similar to the so-called cutting battles in jazz a generation earlier. The sound system competitions, called block parties, were held at local clubs or city parks, where hot-wired street lamps supplied electricity. Bambaataa sometimes mixed sounds from rock-music recordings, bebop jazz records, and television shows into the standard disco and funk beats that Herc relied upon. Eventually, any sound source was considered acceptable and rap artists borrowed sounds from unimaginable sources.

One of the earliest MCs on the scene, DJ Hollywood originated the practice of delivering extensive rhymes over recorded music – the essence of hip-hop. Soon urban deejays such as Herc, Bambaataa, and DJ Hollywood began to team with so-called rappers, and the shouts developed into rhyming, rhythmic patter that was spoken or chanted over the percussive backing music, which came to be known as hip hop – a term that was originally coined by DJ Hollywood.

Although the term rap is often used interchangeably with hip-hop, the latter term encompasses the street subculture that rap music is simply one part of. The term "hip-hop" derives from one of the earliest phrases used in rap. In addition to rap music, the hip-hop subculture also comprises other forms of expression, including graffiti art and break dancing as well as a unique fashion sense and jargon vocabulary.

Rap vocals characteristically emphasize lyrics and wordplay over melody and harmony, achieving interest through rhythmic complexity and variations in the timing of the words. Lyric themes often deal with human relationships, the so-called "gangsta" lifestyle of black Americans who live in inner cities, and contemporary political concerns or aspects of African American history and heritage. Many rap groups use the form to comment on such social problems as poverty and racism. Some rap performers, such as 2 Live Crew, have generated controversy because their lyrics dealt explicitly and graphically with violence and sex.

Generally speaking, rap music is a genre of R&B that consists of words recited, using declaimed vocals, over a strong rhythm accompaniment track known as a "backing track". In general, backing tracks for rap recordings emphasize rhythmic accompaniment and quality of tone or "timber" rather than harmony. Furthermore, many rap songs lack chord changes altogether, influenced by the highly rhythmic style of funk. Songs often include electronic sampling, "scratching" – a percussion technique that involves running a record needle manually across vinyl records to create rhythmic patterns – and "quick mixing" – combining sound bites as short as a few seconds to create a sound collage.

In 1976 Grandmaster Flash introduced the technique of quick mixing. Quick mixing paralleled the rapid-editing style of TV ads used at the time. Shortly after Flash introduced quick mixing, his partner Grandmaster Melle Mel wrote the first extended stories in rhymed rap. Up to this point, most of the words heard over the work of DJs had been improvised phrases, jokes and slang expressions. In 1978 DJ Grand Wizard Theodore introduced the technique of scratching to produce rhythmic sound effects.

Small, independent record labels made the earliest rap records. Rap finally reached the radio airwaves in 1979 when the first two rap records appeared, recorded by the Fatback Band and the Sugar Hill Gang. A series of verses recited by the three members of Sugar Hill Gang, *Rapper's Delight* became a national novelty hit, cracking the Top 40 on the USA pop music charts. The spoken content, mostly rodomontade sprinkled with fantasy, was derived largely from a collection of material used by most of the earlier rappers. The new term hip-hop can be found on the recording. The backing track for *Rapper's Delight* was supplied by hired studio musicians, who replicated the basic groove of the 1979 hit song *Good Times* by the disco band Chic. Perceived as novel by many white Americans, *Rapper's Delight* quickly inspired 1980's *Rapture* by the new-wave band Blondie, as well as a number of other popular records by white artists. *The Breaks* of 1980 by Kurtis Blow also helped to spread rap's popularity among a wider audience.

In 1982 computer-generated sound from synthesizers, including an electronic drum machine began to be employed along with bits and pieces from preexisting recordings. In that same year, Afrika Bambaataa's *Planet Rock* became the first rap record to use synthesizers and a programmable drum machine. With this recording, rap musicians began to create their own backing tracks. A year later Bambaataa introduced the sampling potential of synthesizers on *Looking for the Perfect Beat*.

With the arrival of digital technology in 1983, sampling began to replace the turntable style of cutting and mixing. Sampling eventually facilitated the layering of "found sound" – sound that is captured for later use – enabling rap artists such as Public Enemy to place up to eight samples layered on top of each other. Herc was the first to effectively deconstruct and reconstruct found sound, using the turntable as a musical instrument. In conjunction with sampling and programmed beats, rappers sometimes used live instrumentalists in creating backing tracks.

During the mid-1980s, rap moved from the fringes of hip-hop culture to the mainstream of the North American music industry as white musicians began to take up the new genre. Rap grew popular and reached mainstream audiences in 1986 with hits *You Gotta Fight for Your Right To Party!* by the Beastie Boys, and *Walk This Way* by Run-DMC, who collaborated on a cover version of the song with hard rock band Aerosmith. Known for incorporating rock music into its raps, Run-DMC became one of the first rap groups to be featured regularly on MTV, creating a new audience for rap among white, suburban, middle-class rock fans. Also during the mid-80s, the first female rap group, Salt-N-Pepa, scored several hit singles. By the end of the 80s, MTV had created a program dedicated fully to rap, and performers such as M. C. Hammer and the Beastie Boys who had achieved multi-platinum record sales to broad interracial audiences.

Much early rap was primarily concerned with a dance and party spirit. However in 1982, Grandmaster Flash and the Furious Five took a harder look at social issues in its portrayal of black inner-city life. Their groundbreaking song *The Message* opened the door for the angry, militant style of rap. Other groups followed this example and began taking advantage of the political power of the spoken word. These groups blurred the line between music and politics, using rap to speak directly of the rebellious mood of the disenfranchised. Aggressive, and sometimes misogynist, militant rap in turn influenced so-called gangster or "gangsta" rap, which graphically attempts to depict the brutal scene of urban drug dealers and gang violence.

In the late 1980s a large segment of rap became politicized, resulting in the most overt social agenda in pop music since the urban folk movement of the 60s. This kind of rap soon spread throughout the world and remains influential at present. One could argue that rap has replaced rock music as the creative force in modern popular music. But the lyrics of some rap songs have caused controversy, sometimes promoting and glorifying bigotry, racism, violence, and contempt for women. Defenders of rap lyrics argue that no matter who is listening to the music, the raps are justified because they accurately portray life's realities in urban North America.

The groups Boogie Down Productions and Public Enemy best

exemplified this political style of rap. Public Enemy and their lead singer, Chuck D., came to prominence with their 1988 landmark album *It Takes a Nation of Millions to Hold Us Back*, and the theme song *Fight the Power* from the 1989 film *Do the Right Thing*, by African American filmmaker Spike Lee. They continued to reach a receptive audience with their 1990 follow-up album *Fear of a Black Planet*.

Alongside the rise of political rap came the introduction of gangsta rap, which portrays an outlaw lifestyle of sex, illicit drugs, and violence in urban North America. In 1988 the first major album of gangsta rap, entitled *Straight Outta Compton*, was released by the rap group NWA aka Niggaz With Attitude. Tracks from the album spawned a lot of controversy and generated protests from numerous mainstream community organizations. However, attempts to censor gangsta rap only served to publicize the music and make it more attractive to teenagers. NWA launched the solo careers of some of the most important and influential rappers and rap producers in the gangsta genre.

Among the earliest rap acts to make overtly political and militant statement were Ice Cube, Dr. Dre, KRS-One and Eazy-E. They popularized a style of rap that was uncompromising, militant, radical, and emphasized gunplay and other outlaw aspects of urban life. As rap became increasingly part of the North American mainstream in the 1990s, political rap became less prominent while gangsta rap grew in popularity. Tragically, several gangsta rappers have succumbed to the violent code of guns and death feuds vividly described in their music, including two popular artists, Tupac Shakur and The Notorious B.I.G., who were shot and killed within six months of each other in 1996-97.

Originally confined to black neighborhoods in New York City, rap broke further into the mainstream with the popularity of such performers as L.L. Cool J and Will Smith. They kept the genre open and upbeat, moving toward the so-called "alternative" rap of De La Soul, the Fugees featuring Lauryn Hill, TLC, and others whose work was made accessible to wide audiences through the fusion of rap, pop, and soul. In 1999, rap artists began to win the major American music awards including the Grammy awards.

Recently, many different rap styles have gained mass popularity. Rap has developed into a significant musical and fashion force for listeners around the world, and dance became a big part of the show for many performers. Music styles encompassed hard rock, collages of record samples, and variations on older songs. The genre became increasingly eclectic, demonstrating a limitless capacity to draw samples from any musical forms. In Britain, jazz-rap evolved into a genre known as trip-hop, the leading artists being Tricky and Massive Attack. A number of rap artists, including Guru and US3, borrowed from jazz, using samples as well as live music to produce popular jazz-rap recordings. The group Arrested Development found a rap audience with its reggae and folk-influenced sound. Other popular rappers covering the gambit of styles have included Gang Starr, Ice-T, Coolio, Geto Boys, Snoop Doggy Dogg, Queen Latifah, Puff Daddy aka P. Diddy, Mary J. Blige, Missy Elliot, Jay-Z, Ludacris, 50 Cent, and many others.

Over the past two decades, rap music has developed and influenced both black and white culture in North America. Much of the jargon of hip-hop culture has become standard parts of the slang-vocabulary of millions of teenagers and young adults of various ethnic origins. The hip-hop subculture of rap introduced words, once virtually unknown outside of North America inner-city communities, to the international lexicon. Rap also functions as a voice for these communities, who often do not have access to the mainstream media. In certain circles, rap serves to encourage self-pride and improvement, communicating a positive and fulfilling sense of black history. Black artist Kirk Franklin; hoping to inject an optimistic, constructive, and religious message into rap music, blends gospel influences with hip hop.

Rap has had a great influence on white youth in North America and has helped broaden this group's awareness of black history, heritage, traditions, and culture. Ironically, a white American rapper from the inner-city "8 mile" section of Detroit, Eminem, began the new millennium as the most popular and influential rap artist in the world.

Oscar Peterson

The Guess Who, Bachman Turner Overdrive

Joni Mitchell

Neil Young

Anne Murray

Gordon Lightfoot

clockwise from top left: Barenaked Ladies, Chilliwack,
Streetheart, Alannah Myles, Triumph, Glass Tiger

Bryan Adams

Alanis Morrisette

Céline Dion

10. CANADIAN POPULAR MUSIC

Historically, Canadian radio and television has provided cultural links connecting the country's distant population centers. Canada's vastness and climate had as much to do with the musical and lyrical tone of Canadian music as its regional divisions and isolation, which produced music of distinctly different character in the West Coast, the prairies, central Canada, French-speaking Canada, and the Maritimes. In the past, Canadian popular-music artists looked to the United States as the primary market for their music, with several actually immigrating South of the border. In fact, some of the most perceptive commentaries on American life have come from the songs composed by Canadian artists. By the 1970s, however, a few Canadian artists demonstrated that it was possible to reach an international audience from a Canadian base. In part, this was made possible by the Canadian Radio-Television and Telecommunications Commission (CRTC) requirement of thirty percent Canadian content on all radio stations operating in Canada. A thriving Canadian pop-music industry emerged in the 1980s and continues to make its mark and flourish on the world stage at present.

Canadians had been making significant contributions to the development of recorded pop music since the late nineteenth century. Recording pioneer Thomas Alva Edison, son of a Canadian expatriate, used a wax cylinder to play back the words *Mary had a little lamb* in 1877. In 1886, Edison designed an improved phonograph (meaning Voice-writer) that he demonstrated at the Toronto Industrial Exhibition. There, he recorded the first record in existence, the voice of the governor general of Canada, Lord Stanley – from whom hockey's holy grail gets its name, the Stanley Cup.

Canadian resident Alexander Graham Bell, inventor of the telephone, also collaborated on the development of the wax cylinder playing graphophone in 1880 and founded the American Graphophone Company in 1887.

German immigrant Émile Berliner, interested in acoustics and electricity, designed an improved microphone for the telephone in Washington D.C. in 1877. Ten years later, he patented the gramophone and in 1893 established the U.S. Gramophone Company, which eventually became the giant EMI Corporation. Together with his brother Joseph, he founded, in 1898, Deutsche Grammophon Gesellschaft in his native city of Hanover. There he built the first factory in the world for the exclusive manufacture of records. Within a decade, the company was producing several million records a year. After moving from Washington to the city of Montreal, Émile and his son, Herbert, set up a record company and pressing plant that recorded and manufactured their rubber gramophone discs worldwide. Berliner's company was one of the three most important in North America.

In 1909, Hebert Berliner bought the rights to the "His Master's Voice" logo, later the universally recognized "Nipper" trademark of RCA Records, and established the Compo Company in Lachine, Quebec, the first North American independent record label. Berliner also initiated the first system for distributing records independently and, in 1925, introduced the first electronically recorded disc. The same year Compo issued the first electronically recorded "live" album, a local religious service.

Other Canadian recording and broadcasting pioneers include Reginald Lessened, who transmitted a radio signal to ships at sea in 1901, first broadcast AM radio, invented the wireless telephone, and, in 1919, developed a forerunner of the first television. Colin W. McKenzie of Whitehorse patented the first two-sided gramophone disc in 1909. Montreal based Victor Records introduced the first two-sided disc in 1923, fourteen years after McKenzie's patent application. Working out of Montreal, Italian inventor Galileo Macroni laid claim to establishing the first radio station, XWA, in 1919. Mary Pickford, Canadian-born sweetheart of the silent pictures, became 25 per-cent founder of United Artists Motion Picture Company with Charlie Chaplin, D.W. Griffith, and Douglas Fairbanks, Senior, in 1919.

Along with music industry innovators and moguls, Canada also produced many pop music celebrities during the first half of the twentieth century, leading up to the advent of rock and roll. Comedienne Bea Lillie was in the cast recording of Berlin's *Watch Your Step and Cheap* during WWI. Songwriter Shelton Brooks was responsible for the popular tunes *Darktown Stutter's Ball* and Sophie Tucker's *Some Of These Days*. Bandleader Guy Lombardo's Royal Canadians Orchestra recorded the best-known rendition of *Auld Lang Syne*. Wilf Carter's, aka Montana Slim, country repertoire included the celebrated *Love Knot In My Lariat*.

The success and acclaim earned for Canadian music often came at the personal expense of having to record, tour or live outside the country. The sparse population and the regional nature of the country hindered Canadian musicians. Until the mid-1950s country performers relied on live radio programs, extensive touring in bars, nightclubs, barn dances and local television appearances to earn a living. With a dearth of places to perform and the lack of top-level recording studios, many post-WWII Canadian musicians moved to the United States.

Some of these artists included Maynard Ferguson, a talented jazz instrumentalist whose fame spread worldwide beginning in the 1950s. Virtuoso pianist Oscar Peterson became the most respected and honored jazz musician Canada has produced. Composer, producer, multi-instrumentalist Moe Koffman won fame as one of Canada's most revered jazz veterans. Country performer and writer Hank Snow became a popular fixture of Nashville's *Grand Ol' Opry*. Giselle MacKenzie became well known as a musician and pop singer regular on the 1950s American television show *Your Hit Parade*. Broadway actor, heartthrob, and balladeer Robert Goulet was the long-standing star of the musical *Camelot*, and briefly a cast member of American TV's *Howdy Doody Show*. Singer and songwriter Ray Griff overcame a difficult childhood to become one of Canada's more successful country songwriters. Stu Phillips helped establish the creative role of the producer in rock and roll during the early 60s. The versatile Ronnie Prophet was a country music singer, a gifted impressionist, an entertaining storyteller and an emcee. He was born in Calumet, Quebec.

Canada's domestic media had roots in Canada's diverse culture, and most of its entertainers were imitations of American stars, creating a pattern that endured into the early 1980s – with the notable exception of country artist Stompin' Tom Connors. Canadian television, for example, produced popular musical entertainers such as jazzman Wally Koster and big band singer Juliette. Tommy Ambrose's 1959 TV variety show ran for four years, while Tommy Hunter's television show of the same name began in 1962 and ran until 1989, making it the longest-running network country music show in the world. Television success also blessed the middle-of-the-road folk/pop group The Irish Rovers.

Percy Faith was a musician at the Canadian Broadcasting Corporation (CBC) who became a conductor and composer for Columbia Records in the 1930s and whose biggest hit song was *Theme From A Summer Place* in 1960. Lucille Starr's first album *The French Song* brought her international acclaim when songs on the album began soaring up record charts around the world. The Four Lads were a Toronto singing quartet that first garnered notice backing Johnny Ray on the 1952 hit *Cry*. The Lads' biggest success occurred on the eve of rock and roll in 1955. The foursome's hits included *Moments To Remember*, *No Not Much* and *Standing On The Corner*. The group's vocal format put them somewhere between a black R&B doo-wop group and a barbershop quartet. Two more popular Canadian acts, The Diamonds and the Crew Cuts, followed in the Lad's footsteps towards the approaching rock and roll revolution.

In 1956 American Rock and Roll hit Canada like a hurricane. By the late 1950s, Canada began producing its own Elvis Presley hopefuls. The first Canadian popstar of the new rock era was Ottawa's Paul Anka, who struck gold with the classic *Diana*, a 1957 song inspired by a crush on his babysitter that was written when he was just sixteen years old. Without the standard good looks of a teen idol, he instead had versatility and the talent to write and produce his own songs; assets that saw him nurture a long career. Anka composed the pop classic *My Way* in 1968 and the theme music for NBC-TV's *The Tonight Show*.

Rock and roll made its official entry into Canada in 1958 with the arrival in Toronto of an Arkansas rockabilly named Romping' Ronnie Hawkins. Hawkins' band The Hawks turned out one experienced, gifted, and influential instrumentalist after another. Most famous were the musicians who made up the early 1960s line-up of The Hawks. They later became one of the most seasoned and brilliant rock ensembles ever under the name The Band, featuring Robbie Robertson. In 1966 The Band left Hawkins to tour with Bob Dylan during his controversial transfiguration from acoustic folk to electric rock and, under Dylan's auspices, they discovered their own talent for songwriting. In 1968-69 The Band released two consecutive albums that bridged rock, gospel, soul, folk, and country roots into a remarkable account of North American folklore. The Band enjoyed success and critical acclaim up until they disbanded following the 1976 concert *The Last Waltz*, one of the best rock documentaries of all time. Robbie Robertson's solo career has produced several reflective albums – delving into his indigenous musical heritage and roots.

During the 1960s Canadian folk singers such as Joni Mitchell, Ian & Sylvia, and Gordon Lightfoot, were among the most celebrated recording artists to have an impact internationally. They also opened doors for several other singer-composers like Murray McLauchlan, Bruce Cockburn, Stan Rogers and Willie P. Bennett. Each, through their songs, communicated a part of the Canadian experience to the world. Strong regional ties and the influence of geography and climate were qualities often shared by Canadian folk singers. Their compositions contributed some of the most identifiable, distinctive, and appreciated Canadian popular music. It is telling that several of these artists had to find success abroad to be appreciated at home. Although some continued living in Canada, several fled to the United States, where they believed their music would be appreciated and would have a better opportunity to be recorded and promoted internationally. Ironically, it was Canadian-born producer Pierre Cossette who, in 1971, organized the first broadcast of America's prestigious Grammy Awards ceremony to a North American television audience.

Expatriates included John Kay of the hard rock group Steppenwolf, Zal Yanovsky of the rock group the Lovin' Spoonful, folk singer Denny Doherty, a member of the wildly successful folk rock quartet the Mamas & the Papas, pop songwriter Andy Kim, songwriter Leonard Cohen, soul singer David Clayton-Thomas and rock nonconformist Neil Young.

Winnipeg-bred Young has proven to be the most enduring and influential of them all. He crashed the California folk and rock scenes in the mid-1960s, first attaining success with pioneering rock band the Buffalo Springfield. He later found greater fame when teaming up with 1960s-70s supergroup Crosby Stills & Nash. He then embarked on an inconsistent but always interesting solo career. Young's many albums reveal that he is comfortable with folk and country music but also ready to explore lesser-known modern styles or to create driving, uncompromising rock and roll. This independent and fearless spirit made him a leader among his contemporaries and a deity to a generation of younger songwriters and rock bands that consider him the godfather of grunge rock.

The most influential Canadian female artist to emerge from the 1960s was, without a doubt, Joni Mitchell. Mitchell remained a solo artist and also became part of the Crosby Stills and Nash entourage. From the courageous confessional writing of her early albums, she explored bolder, more poetic long-form songs and different progressive styles including jazz, becoming a highly colorful and distinctive musician in the process. In the 90s, several female artists cited Mitchell's highly acclaimed albums as inspiration for their own recordings.

In the 1960s, Canadian recording studios and record labels lagged far behind their British or American counterparts. They simply lacked the technology or expertise to compete. Canada's independent record companies mostly serviced small regional markets. The major labels operating in Canada at that time were foreign-owned and generally not interested in investing in Canadian artists. The domestic music industry also had very few off-stage experienced talents such as managers, publicists, and audio technicians. To help alleviate this situation, Montreal recording pioneer David Leonard created Trebas Institute in 1979, offering one of the first comprehensive programs in North America on the art, technology and business of music.

Another challenge during this period was radio airplay. Canadian media in the 1950s and 60s preferred to offer their listeners programming lined with well-known hits by proven American or British artists, often presuming Canadian artists and their recordings to be substandard. This cautious and somewhat prejudicial attitude stunted the potential and growth of the fledgling Canadian music industry. For example, in 1965, a recording of the song *Shakin' All Over* by Winnipeg band Chad Allen and The Expressions was sent to radio stations under the group name The Guess Who? Not knowing the group, many radio station programmers played it, assuming it to be one of the latest bands in the British Invasion. The song went on to become an international success. Now resigned to being The Guess Who, the band toured Canada tirelessly and produced more than a dozen modest hits before meeting gifted Canadian producer Jack Richardson and signing to his production company. With Richardson at the helm, The Guess Who notched a huge international single in 1968 with *These Eyes*, which became the catalyst for a successful career that produced many more hits, including *American Woman, Share The Land, Clap For The Wolfman*, and later solo careers by front men Burton Cummings and Randy Bachman.

The Guess Who's high-rolling career was nevertheless an exception and not the general rule for Canadian talent. The evident lack of support for Canadian musicians at all levels of the pop music industry prompted the CRTC, Canada's equivalent to the American FCC, to adopt rules and regulations requiring AM radio stations to play at least 30% of records classified as Canadian. This groundbreaking classification required that the music or lyrics be written by a Canadian, and the artist be Canadian or the record be produced in Canada. This so-called Canadian Content or "Cancon" ruling came into effect in 1971 and immediately resulted in an increase in record production and opportunities for Canadian talent. That same year, the Canadian Academy of Recording Arts and Science (CARAS) began producing the annual Juno Awards, which was telecast by the CBC to acknowledge and applaud the accomplishments of the Canadian musical entertainment business.

Since 1971, Cancon rules have often been adjusted by the CRTC for changing programming and technological advances, however, the general principals and goals remain the same. Some foreign nations with open airwaves, in particular the United States, do not look favorably on content restrictions. Most Canadians, however, believe this landmark experiment has been extremely successful and boost of its emulation in other countries, such as France.

Canadian songstress Anne Murray was the first Canadian popstar of the Cancon era. Launched by her 1970 multimillion-selling single, *Snowbird*, Murray benefited from the extra airplay in Canada to firmly establish her wonderfully warm, clear vocal style and penchant for light pop, folk and country. Cancon also helped lay the foundation for an impressive international career that has seen Murray record dozens of albums, receive numerous music industry awards and become one of pop music's most recognizable and respected artists.

Internationally, the 1970s was a prosperous time for the music industry and Canada's industry also benefited from a period of unprecedented record sales for domestic recording artists. Many new homegrown bands emerged, most notably in rock, and had varying degrees of success domestically or abroad. Some of these groups included Lighthouse, The Stampeders, Prism, Fludd, Crowbar, Five Man Electrical Band, Triumph, Chilliwack, and Trooper.

One of the most successful Canadian groups in the 1970s, Bachman Turner Overdrive (BTO), also had one of the best and most powerful managers, Bruce Allen. Initially, the Vancouver-based Allen used his high-powered tactics to guide Guess Who-alumni Randy Bachman's BTO to become one of the most popular hard rock acts in the world. By the late 70s, Allen and co-manager Lou Blair had another extremely popular act in Loverboy. In the 80s, Allen discovered his biggest star, Bryan Adams, and by the 90s would also be managing American country star Martina McBride, highly regarded Canadian record producers Bruce Fairbairn and Bob Rock, and Anne Murray.

Another homegrown supergroup born in the 1970s was Rush, skillfully managed by Ray Danniels. Although Danniels managed other acts and also established the independent Toronto-based Anthem label, his greatest and most consistent success has been with Rush, which in turn has proven itself to be a prime example of artistic growth and integrity during a career that has witnessed the band explore heavy metal, progressive-rock, new wave rock, reggae and other styles on the way to selling millions of albums around the world, establishing it as one of rock's most dependable concert attractions.

To completely and properly understand Canadian popular music, one must comprehend its unique and rich bilingual character. A quarter of the Canadian population speaks the language of Molière and thus wishes to be entertained in its mother tongue. Over the past decades a francophone music industry has flourished, centered in "La Belle Province" of Quebec. By the 1970s it was clear that French Canada not only had developed an industry that was insular and culturally in sync with its audience but was growing more apart from its English counterpart. The French Canadian market was then, as now, distinct and self-sustaining.

Although in the 1970s and 80s there were several examples of a French-English crossover by acts such as disco diva Patsy Gallant, rocker Michel Pagliaro, teen television star René Simard, easy listening pianist Andre Gagnon, Franco-Manitoban Daniel Lavoie, or sister folk duo Kate & Anna McGarrigle, surprisingly, few English Canadian popular artists ventured into Quebec to reciprocate. Meanwhile, English-speaking Quebec artists often remained local phenomena with few exceptions, such as hard rock trio Mahogany Rush and concert-mogul Donald Tarlton (DKD) and his Aquarius label's successful exports April Wine, Corey Hart and Sass Jordan.

Most successful French recording musicians were largely unknown in English Canada. These Quebecois artists included the hugely popular Beau Dommage, Offenbach, Octobre, Corbeau, Ginette Reno, Robert Charlebois, Garolou, Jim et Bertrand, and Harmonium.

While the folk music tradition in Quebec dominated throughout the first half of the twentieth century with artists such as La Bolduc, the transition to modern pop and more contemporary songwriting began in the 1950s with the Chansonniers led by Félix Leclerc. Leclerc's emotional style blended Quebecois sentiment with reflections of political and cultural frustrations. When the Quebec recording industry association or ADISQ, created its equivalent of the Junos in 1979, it paid homage to Leclerc by calling its trophies the Félix Awards. Performers who followed Leclerc's path included Jean-Pierre Ferland, Gilles Vigneault, Claude Leveillée, Claude Gauthier, Raymond Lévesque, Renée Claude, and lyricist Luc Plamondon.

French Canadian talent initially responded to the 1960s impact of the British Invasion and Bob Dylan with their own translated versions of Anglo-American hits, as recorded by singing groups like Les Classels, César et les Romains, Les Jérolas, and Les Baronets –featuring Celine Dion's manager and husband René Angelil. Eventually, however, Quebec artists spread their creative wings and developed their own style through the work of such artists as Michel Louvain, Pierre Lalonde, Joel Denis, Donald Lautrec, Michèle Richard, Tony Roman, Renée Claude, Chantal Pary, Willie Lamothe, Johnny Farrago, and René and Nathalie Simard, aptly managed by Quebec's entertainment giant Guy Cloutier.

Vocalists such as Reno, Pagliaro, and Charlebois took Quebecois pop to higher levels of record sales, credibility and artistic merit. Their success helped the industry to feel secure in the strength and uniqueness of its culture, unlike the English side of the Canadian business. An avalanche of acts covering the range of pop, folk, rock, blues, jazz, disco, and rap music soon joined them. A sample of these artists include Boule Noire, Claude Dubois, Richard Séguin, Paul Piché, Jim Corcoran, Gilles Valiquette, Marjo, Laurence Jalbert, New Brunswick's Roch Voisine, and more recently Okoumé, Les Respectables, Noir Silence, Dubmatique, La Chicane, Groovy Aardvark, Jean Leloup, Kevin Parent, Daniel Belanger, Eric Lapointe, Linda Lemay, Marc Dery, Isabelle Boulay, Les Cowboys Fringants, Ariane Moffatt, Daniel Boucher, Bruno Pelletier, France D'Amour, and Sylvain Cossette.

Quebec also showcases its cultural uniqueness via a multitude of eclectic francophone music competitions and annual music festivals. These events spotlight the full spectrum of popular French music styles. For example, the Polliwog Festival provided a window of opportunity for young alternative rock bands with showcases, recordings, and concert tours for almost a decade. Other events include the pop-oriented Granby International Song Festival, Les Francofolies, and Star Académie – Quebec's version of Canadian & American Idol.

Cancon regulations help guarantee radio and television exposure in Quebec-based media. Television, for example, has, over the years, produced numerous musical variety shows and programming for kids. French speaking children are well served by several multi-platinum selling musical acts such as Carmen Campagne, Annie Brocoli, and Patou.

Despite English Canada's many successes during the 1970s, it became apparent that the nation's small population and the continued resistance of radio and other media still created problems for the survival of Canadian independent labels. The lukewarm investment by the major record companies into Canadian talent was, by no means, a guarantee of better quality recordings or easy access to the global market. With Canadian media trying to find ways to program as much Cancon as possible, some acts almost suffered from overexposure. The Canadian pop music industry experienced severe growing pains as a consequence.

On the eve of a new decade, Canada's English language industry struggled once again to find a voice. The late seventies still echoed with the sentimental balladry of Dan Hill's Grammy nominated *Sometimes When We Touch*, while the early eighties confronted the sociological impact of punk and new wave rock. Politically outspoken bands as diverse as Vancouver's Pointed Sticks and DOA or Toronto's Rough Trade and Diodes represented the new, revolutionary spirit of Canadian pop musical culture. These trends and concerns were reflected by Canada's pop music as well. Likewise, there was a whole new generation of performers to lead the way or benefit from these developments. By far, the most successful among them were Bryan Adams and producer-composer David Foster.

Foster, originally from Victoria, British Columbia, made his reputation in Los Angeles as a session musician and conductor. He also was the leader of 1970s studio band Skylark and writer of its hit song Wildflower. As a producer, arranger and writer he won Juno and Grammy awards for his work with Celine Dion, Chicago, Barbra Streisand, Whitney Houston and several others. In 1995 he collaborated with songwriters Bryan Adams, Jim Vallance and Paul Hyde of the Payolas, on the anthem *Tears Are Not Enough*. The song was recorded by Northern Lights, a colossal group effort that brought together the best of Canadian talent, raising millions of dollars for African famine relief. At Live Aid, Adams represented Canada and performed the song in front of a worldwide audience.

The Vancouver-based Adams first achieved million-selling

international record sales with songwriting partner Jim Vallance through such hits as *Cuts Like A Knife, Somebody* and *Diana*. In the 1990s, collaboration with quintessential arena-rock producer Robert John "Mutt" Lange (Shania Twain's producer, co-writer and husband) delivered ever-bigger hits including *(Everything I Do) I Do It For You* and *Have You Ever Really Loved A Woman*.

The 1980s spawned a stronger industry infrastructure that reinforced and capitalized on a newly discovered pride in Canada's increasingly sophisticated and innovative music. Managers, publicists, audio technicians and recording studios attained a high level of international credibility. Other positive elements included successful publishers and independent labels, notably the CanCon successes Attic and Nettwerk, a multitude and variety of trade media, and government or corporate funding programs including the Fund to Assist Canadian Talent On Record (FACTOR), VideoFACT, and the Canada Council.

As the decade played out, new acts joined the now vibrant Canadian scene. Across the country, Canadian music became fashionable as a result of recordings by artists from across the country including Streetheart, Skinny Puppy, Doug And The Slugs, Headpins, Barney Bentall, Colin James, Grapes Of Wrath, and Sons Of Freedom from the west coast; Northern Pikes, The Pursuit Of Happiness, and k.d. Lang from the Prairies; Red Rider, Jane Siberry, Kim Mitchell, Honeymoon Suite, Glass Tiger, Platinum Blonde, The Jeff Healey Band, The Nylons, and Alannah Myles from Ontario; Luba, Gino Vanelli, Men Without Hats, The Box, Oliver Jones, and thrash metal band Voivod from Quebec; Haywire and Minglewood from the Maritimes.

Spearheading the integration of rapidly changing technology and multi-media to the benefit of Canada's music industry during the 1980s was Canadian media entrepreneur Moses Znaimer's MuchMusic TV channel and its francophone equivalent, MusiquePlus. Initially relying on pop-rock video clips, MuchMusic's on-air birth in 1985 not only connected regional activities to the rest of the country but also united its many diverse performers and, by focusing on new, emerging acts, created many new popstars.

Canadian English language pop entered the 1990s on a wave of national pride, much stronger and diverse than ever before. The impact of acid jazz, rap, hip-hop, techno and ever-evolving variations and mutations on dance music had been experienced mostly in the large urban centers, particularly in Vancouver, Toronto and Montreal; each with their rapidly growing population of Asian and black immigrants. Domestically, Bass Is Base, Maestro Fresh Wes, Kish, and other similar acts have netted hit records with these new styles. Aboriginal music from such admired indigenous artists as Susan Aglukark, Wapistan, Jerry Alfred, and Quebec's Kashtin, also enriched the character of Canadian music.

The French language music industry in the 1990s continued as a reflection of Canadian politics in that it remained distinct, yet it yielded many of the nation's biggest superstars, including Celine Dion. Dion was initially a child star in Quebec, recording in her native French. Lured to CBS Records Canada in 1986 by Bill Rotari, manager René Angelil struck a deal that allowed her to quickly score several international English hits while continuing to successfully record in French. Dion's charming personality, diva-like singing and selection of polished, commercial romantic ballads and danceable pop has since sold millions of albums and earned her numerous Félix, Juno, Grammy and Oscar awards.

The 1990s also witnessed the arrival of the Maritimes music industry. Like Quebec, the provinces of New Brunswick, Nova Scotia, Prince Edward Island, and Newfoundland had developed in isolation; its biggest star of the past three decades being Springhill and Anne Murray. In the past two decades, its main influence was folk songwriter Stan Rogers. More recently, the timid Rita MacNeil became its most unlikely star. A shy blues-influenced folk singer, MacNeil found favor with many Canadians both with her recordings and on her weekly variety television series. Other maritime acts with strong roots in Canadian folk and traditional music included Lenny Gallant, the Barra MacNeils, and the Rankin Family, whose records cleverly blended country, rock, and the region's Celtic lore. With roots of a different kind, punk-influenced bands such as Eric's Trip, Sloan, Jale, and Hardship Post awakened Canada to an untapped goldmine of new rock talent. Finally, providing a shocking link between Maritime folk tradition and modern rock was kilted fiddle player Ashley MacIsaac, who unexpectedly provided Canadians with the freshest and most eclectic recordings in years.

In the 1990s Canadian country music finally hit its stride with the strong crossover feeling to such new artists as Michelle Wright, George Fox, Charlie Major, Quartette, Colleen Peterson, Blue Shadows, Paul Brandt, Cassandra Vassik, Lori Yates, Patricia Conroy, and international megastar Shania Twain. The Canadian Country Music Association, established in 1975 as the Academy of Country Music Entertainment, has sponsored an annual country music week in different cities across Canada. Country Music Week and Big Country Awards have brought performers and industry folks together and have become key events in the development of country music. The Country Music Association is also responsible for the annual Country Music Awards and Canadian Country Music Hall of Honor.

At present there are numerous new Canadian recording acts of all types traveling up, down, and across the Great White North in rusty vehicles loaded with their instruments, selling new self-released compact discs or signed to maverick and street smart independent labels, licensing their indie music to different territories around the globe, marketing themselves on the Internet, and building a fan-base. This vibrant indie circuit helped develop, in the past, such acts as I, Mother Earth, Tom Cochrane, Jann Arden, Crash Test Dummies, 54-40, Blue Rodeo, Tragically Hip, Moist, Grim Skunk, Hayden, Me Mom and Morgantaler, The Watchmen, Bran Van 3000, Treble Charger, Anonymus, Merlin, and many others.

As the twenty-first century picks up steam, The Canadian music industry must now face the various challenges presented by the dilemmas and opportunities created by rapidly changing technology. These take the form of copyright ownership in the face of digitized music carriers; the communication, dissemination, misappropriation and illegal downloading via the Internet; and the ongoing issue of whether Canada still requires content regulations.

Esteemed international artists such as Bryan Adams, Celine Dion, Alanis Morissette, Avril Lavigne, Diana Krall, Sarah McLachlan, Barenaked Ladies, and Shania Twain have collectively sold millions of records and hundreds of thousands of concert tickets, garnered industry awards, and merited popular global recognition by exporting a cultural seam of the Canadian fabric. Their worldwide impact has only enhanced the commercial viability of other Canadian artists. It is, however, the domestic popularity of today's diverse Canuck talents that suggests Canadian pop music has matured and is appreciated for its own character and quality at home. These performers are speaking directly to Canadians with passion and enthusiasm about experiences that touch them and yet have universal appeal and resonance.

AC/DC

EPILOGUE

Upon completion of this fascinating and stimulating musical voyage, I cannot help but restate that this treatise was only a general overview of the topic. Many more volumes are needed to do justice to the evolution of this popular art form.

It is difficult to arrive at an objective description of an evolutionary movement while it is in progress, only a period of time can provide the necessary perspective. It can be acknowledged, however, that music has never before passed through a more turbulent phase than in the last century. The great number and diversity of stylistic distinctions has precluded a trademark designation for modern pop music.

Despite the disproportionate attention often given to the most radical musical experiments, the majority of leading composers working at present continue along the moderate path established in the late 1920s and 30s. And, if one can rely on the lessons of history, the mainstream of music will continue to absorb those new techniques that contribute to expressiveness and communication while discarding that which is merely novel and sensational, so that music history will remain an evolutionary rather than a revolutionary process.

The ever-changing and evolving chronicle of popular music remains the story of its creators and listeners. Future audiences should not forget or ignore this epic saga but instead embrace the richness of its truly human character and vision. If music nourishes a person's soul and brings us together as a people then the heritage of that music must be understood and passed on to those who will, in the future, live its history.

The story of modern popular music continues to be told every day, with every new artist, song, and style warmly received by appreciative audiences.

As for the future of modern pop music? ... let's all sit back, listen, and enjoy the sounds.

Thanks for the read,
Mark Vinet

1st row: Supertramp
2nd row: Styx
3rd row: Queen
4th row: Rush

BIBLIOGRAPHY, NOTES & SOURCES

African American Biography. 4 vols. Gale Research, 1994.

Africans in America: America's Journey Through Slavery. Educational Foundation, 1998.

Alexander, Stella, *Quaker Testimony Against Slavery & Racial Discrimination: An Anthology.* 1958.

Alvin D. McCurdy Collection, *Preserving Black History.* Archives of Ontario. Toronto, Canada.

Archives Nationales du Québec. Montreal, Quebec, Canada.

Archives of Ontario. Toronto, Ontario, Canada.

Arnold, Denis. *The New Oxford Companion to Music*, 2 vol. Oxford University Press, 1983, reprint 1990.

Association of Canadian Archivists. Ottawa, Ontario, Canada.

Atlantic Monthly Press, *One Hundred Nineteen Years of the Atlantic.* 1977.

Bailyn, B., *The Peopling of British North America.* 1986.

Baines, Anthony. *The Oxford Companion to Musical Instruments.* Oxford University Press, 1992.

Baker, Theodore. *Baker's Biographical Dictionary of Musicians*, 8th ed., rev. Nicolas Slonimsky, 1992.

Ball, Edward. *Slaves in the Family.* Farrar, Straus & Giroux, 1998.

Balliett, Whitney. *American Musicians II: Seventy-two Portraits in Jazz.* 2nd ed. Oxford Univ. Pr., 1996.

Barlow, William. *Looking Up at Down: The Emergence of Blues Culture.* Temple Univ. Press, repr. 1990.

Bartok, Bela. *Hungarian Folk Music.* Oxford, 1931, reprinted by Hyperion, 1986.

Baskerville, David. *The Music Business Handbook & Career Guide, 6th & 7th eds.* Sage Pub. 1995, 2001.

Batten, Joseph. *Joe Batten's Book: The Story of Sound Recording* (1956).

Bierley, Paul E. *John Philip Sousa: American Phenomenon.* Warner Brothers Publications, 2001.

Bell, Winthrop P. The *"Foreign Protestants" and the Settlement of Nova Scotia.* Acadiensis, 1992.

Berendt, Joachim. *The Jazz Book*, rev. ed. Chicago Review, 1982, 6th ed. 1992.

Berger, Melvin. *The Story of Folk Music.* S.G. Phillips, 1976.

Bergeron, Leandre. *The history of Quebec: A Patriot's Handbook.* NC Press, 1971.

Berklee College of Music. Boston, Massachusetts, USA.

Berlin, Ira, and others, eds. *Free at Last: A Documentary History of Slavery, Freedom, and the Civil War.* New Pr., 1992; Slaves Without Masters: The Free Negro in the Antebellum South. 1974; 1981.

Bertley, Leo W. *Canada and Its People of African Descent.* Pierrefonds: Bilongo Publishers, 1977.

Bianconi, Lorenzo *Music in the Seventeenth Century.* Cambridge University Press, 1987.

Bibliothèque de l'Université de Montréal. Montreal, Quebec, Canada.

Bibliothèque de Montréal. Montréal, Quebec, Canada.

Bibliothèque de Québec. Quebec City, Quebec, Canada.

Bibliothèque nationale de France. Paris, France.

Bibliothèque nationale du Québec. Montreal, Quebec, Canada.

Billboard 100th Anniversary Issue: 1894-1994 & Billboard International Buyer's Guide, BPI Com. 1994.

Bilodeau, R., Comeau, R., Gosselin, A., Julien, D., *Historie Des Canadas*, Hurtubise HMH.

Bindas, Kenneth J., ed. *America's Musical Pulse: Popular Music in 20th Century Society.* Praeger, 1992.

Black Canadian Studies, Dalhousie University Libraries. Halifax, Nova Scotia, Canada.

Blassingame, John W. *The Slave Community: Plantation Life in the Ante-Bellum South.* Oxford Pr. 1979.

Blocher, Arlo. *Folk.* Troll, 1976.

Blues Archives, University of Mississippi Library.

Blume Friedrich ed., *Die Musik in Geschichte und Gegenwart*, 17 vol. (1949-86);

Bogdanov, V. ed. et al. *All Music Guide to Rock: Definitive Guide to Rock, Pop, Soul, R&B, & Rap* and *All Music Guide to Hip-Hop: Definitive Guide to Rap & Hip-Hop.* Backbeat Bks, 2003.

Bohlman, Philip V., *The Study of Folk Music in the Modern World (Folkloristics)*, Indiana Univ. Pr, 1988.

Botermans, Jack, and others. *Making and Playing Musical Instruments.* Washington, 1989.

Botkin, B. A., editor. *Lay My Burden Down: A Folk History of Slavery.* Reprint, Delta, 1994.

Bowman, Rob and M. J. *Soulsville U.S.A: The Story of Stax Records.* Schirmer Books 2003.

British Archives & British Museum. London, United Kingdom.

Broughton, Simon. World Music, Volumes 1 & 2. Rough Guide, 2000.

Broven, John. *Rhythm & Blues in New Orleans.* Pelican Pub Co, Reprint edition 1983.

Brown, Charles T., *Country and Western Music.* Prentice Hall Trade, 1985.

Brown, Howard Mayer. *Music in the Renaissance* (1976) The Prentice Hall History of Music Series;

Bufwack, M., & Oermann, R. K. *Finding Her Voice: The Saga of Women in Country Music.* Crown, 1993.

Bukofzer, Manfred F. *Music in the Baroque Era, from Monteverdi to Bach*, W.W. Norton 1947, reissued 1977; *Studies in Medieval and Renaissance Music*, W.W. Norton, 1964.

Burns, Ken and Ward, Geoffrey C. *Jazz: A History of America's Music*. Alfred A. Knopf, Random House Audio books; *Jazz*, A Film by Ken Burns. Florentine Films, 2000.

Canadian Conference of the Arts, Directory of the Arts, Ottawa, Canada.

Canadian Country Music Association (CCMA). Woodbridge, Ontario, Canada.

Canadian Folk Music Journal. Canadian Journal for Traditional Music, 1989.

Canadian Heritage, Parks Canada. Ottawa, Ontario, Canada.

Canadian National Edition. McClelland & Stewart Inc. 1999.

Cantwell, Robert, *When We Were Good: The Folk Revival*. Harvard University Press, 1997.

Careless, J.M.S. ed., Colonists & Canadians, 1760-1867, 1971, repr. 1980.

Carlin, Richard. *English and American Folk Music*. Facts on File, 1987.

Carr, Ian and others. *Jazz: The Essential Companion*. Prentice, 1988.

Carter, William. *Preservation Hall: Music from the Heart*. Norton, 1991.

Catton, Bruce. *The Civil War*. Houghton Mifflin Company. 1960, 1988.

Center for Popular Music, Middle Tennessee State University.

Charters, Samuel. B., *Jazz: New Orleans, 1885-1963: An Index to the Negro Musicians of New Orleans (The Roots of Jazz)*, Da Capo 1963, repr. 1983.

Clark, Dick, and Shore, Michael. *History of American Bandstand: It's Got a Great Beat and You Can Dance to It*. Ballantine Books, 1987; with Fred Bronson, *Dick Clark's American Bandstand*. HarperCollins, 1997.

Clarke, Donald. *The Penguin Encyclopedia of Popular Music*. Viking, 1989.

Collier, J.L. *The Making of Jazz*. Dell, 1979.

Columbia University Libraries and Research Centers. New York, New York, USA.

Comotti, Giovanni *Music in Greek and Roman Culture*. 1989; originally published in Italian, 1979.

Conrad, Margaret, *History of the Canadian Peoples*, 2 vols. Addison-Wesley Pub Co., 1993.

Copyright Law of the United States of America and Related Laws. Superintendent of Documents, Washington DC, USA.

Cougle, Jim. *Canadian Blood American Soil: The Story of Canada's Contribution to the American Civil War*. The Civil War Heritage Society of Canada, 1994.

Country Music Foundation. *Country: The Music and the Musicians: Pickers, Slickers, Cheatin' Hearts*. Superstars Abbeville, 1988; *Superstars: The Music and the Musicians*. 2nd ed. Abbeville, 1994.

Country Music Magazine, ed. *The Comprehensive Country Music Encyclopedia*. Timeless, 1994.

Cowper and Newton Museum. Olney, Buckinghamshire UK England.

Creighton, Helen. *Songs and Ballads from Nova Scotia*. Dover Publishing, 1932, reprint 1992.

Crouch, Stanley. *In Depth* interview, C-SPAN Book TV. 2003; with Quincy McCoy, *No Static: A Guide to Creative Radio Programming*. Backbeat Books, 2002.

Curtis, Jim. *Rock Eras: Interpretations of Music and Society, 1954-1984*. Popular Press, 2003.

Dahl, Linda. *Stormy Weather: The Music and Lives of a Century of Jazzwomen*. Limelight, 1989.

Daniel, Ralph Thomas, contributor, *The Harvard Brief Dictionary of Music*. Fine Comms. repr. ed. 1997.

Davies, Norman. *Europe: A History*. Oxford University Press, 1996.

Davis, Francis. *Outcats: Jazz Composers, Instrumentalists, and Singers*. Oxford University Press, 1990.

Daw, S. *The Music of Johann Sebastian Bach, the Choral Works*. Fairleigh Dickinson Univ. Press, 1981.

Dawidoff, Nicholas. *In the Country of Country: People and Places in American Music*. Pantheon, 1997.

De Lisle, Tim. *Lives of the Great Songs*. Trafalgar Square, 1995.

De Toledano, R., ed., *Frontiers of Jazz*, 3d ed. Ungar Pub Co., 1978, 1994.

Dearling, Robert, ed. *The Illustrated Encyclopedia of Musical Instruments*. Schirmer, 1996.

DeCurtis, Anthony, eds. *Rolling Stone Illustrated History of Rock & Roll*. 3rd ed. Random House, 1992.

Dellar, Fred, & Cackett, Alan, *The Harmony Illustrated Encyclopedia of Country Music*, Crown 1987.

Diagram Group. *Musical Instruments of the World: An Illustrated Encyclopedia*. Sterling, 1997.

Downs, Philip G. *Anthology of Classical Music*. W.W. Norton, 1992.

Duckles, Vincent and Zimmerman, Franklin B. *Words to Music*. 1967.

Eccles, W. J. *The Canadian Frontier, 1534-1821*. Rev. ed. 1983; and, France in America. 1972.

Edgar, Walter. *South Carolina: A History*. University of South Carolina Press, 1998.

Ellison, Curtis W. *Country Music Culture: From Hard Times to Heaven*. Univ. Press of Mississippi, 1995.

Elrod, Bruce C. *Your Hit Parade and American Top Ten Hits: A Week-by-Week Guide to the Nation's Favorite Music, 1935-1994*. 4th ed. Popular Culture, 1994.

Eltis, David. *The Rise of African Slavery in the Americas*. Cambridge University Press, 1999.

Emerson, Ken. *Doo-Dah: Stephen Foster and the Rise of American Popular Culture*. Da Capo Pr, 1998.

Emmett, Dan, Bruce, G. B. *The Drummers' and Fifers' Guide* (Civil War). WM. A. Pond, NY, 1865.

Erlewine, Michael, ed. *All Music Guide to Jazz*. 2nd ed. Miller Freeman, 1996.

Feather, Leonard. The New Edition of the Encyclopedia of Jazz. 1962; repr. Da Capo, 1984; *The Passion for Jazz* 1990; *The Encyclopedia Yearbooks of Jazz*. Horizon, 1956. Reprint. Da Capo, 1993.

Fennell, Frederick. *The Sound of the Civil War*. Mercury, 1990.

Festival International de Jazz de Montreal. *Montreal Festival: A Jazz Celebration*. Spectra, 1996.

Filler, Louis, *Crusade against Slavery*. ed. by Keith Irvine, 2d rev. ed. 1986.

Forucci, S.L. *A Folk Song History of America: America Through Its Songs* Prentice Hall, 1984.

Fowke, Edith, ed. *The Penguin Book of Canadian Folk Songs*. Penguin, 1987; with A. Mills, *Singing our History: Canada's Story in Song*. 1984; with R. Johnston, *Folk Songs of Canada, I & II*. 1954 & 67.

Franklin, John Hope, Schweninger, L. *Runaway Slaves: Rebels on the Plantation*. Oxford Univ. Pr, 2000; with Alfred Moss, *From Slavery to Freedom: A History of African Americans*. McGraw-Hill, 1997.

Friedwald, Will. *Jazz Singing: America's Great Voices from Bessie Smith to Bebop & Beyond*. Collier 92.

Friends World Committee for Consultation, Handbook of the Religious Society of Friends, 5th ed. 1967.

Friesen, Gerald. *The Canadian Prairies: A History*. 1984. Reprint. Univ. of Toronto Pr., 1987.

Gaisberg, Fred. *The Music Goes Round*. (history of the phonograph), Ayer Co Pub, 1942, reprinted 1977.

Gammond, Peter. *The Oxford Companion to Popular Music*. Oxford, 1991.

Gates, Henry Louis, Jr, ed. *The Classic Slave Narratives*. New American Library, 1987; with Appiah, Kwame Anthony, Eds. *Africana: The Encyclopedia of the African and African American Experience*. Basic Civitas Books, 1999; *Wonders of the African World*. Random House, 1998; with West, Cornel. *The African-American Century: How Black Americans Have Shaped Our Century*. Free Press, 2000.

Geiringer, Karl. *Instruments in the History of Western Music*. 3rd ed. Oxford University Press, 1978.

Gelatt, Roland. *The Fabulous Phonograph: 1877-1977*. MacMillan Publishing Co., 2nd rev. ed. 1977.

George, Nelson, *Hip Hop America*. Penguin, 1999; *The Death of Rhythm and Blues*. Penguin, 2003.

Gilder Lehrman Institute of American History. The Gilder Lehrman Collection, Pierpont Morgan.

Gilmore, J. *Swinging in Paradise: The Story of Jazz in Montreal*. 1987.

Gioia, Ted. *The History of Jazz*. Oxford Press, 1997.

Ginell, Cary. *Milton Brown and the Founding of Western Swing*. University of Illinois Press, 1994.

Gitler, Ira. *Jazz Masters of the Forties*. Da Capo, 1982; *Swing to Bop: An Oral History of the Transition in Jazz in the 1940's*. Oxford University Press, 1987.

Goertzen, Valerie Woodring, *Folk Music*. Univ. of North Carolina, Greensboro.

Goldsmith, Peter D., *Making People's Music: Moe Asch and Folkways Records*. 1998.

Goodman, Fred. *The Mansion on the Hill: Dylan, Young, Geffen, Springsteen, and the Head-On Collision of Rock and Commerce*. Times Books, 1997.

Gordon, Robert. *Can't Be Satisfied: The Life and Times of Muddy Waters*. Back Bay Books, 2003.

Grant, Mary H. *Private Woman, Public Person: An Account of the Life of Julia Ward Howe from 1819 to 1868*. Carlson Pub., 1994.

Green, Richard. *Country and Western Music*. Cdn 2000 National Ed., McClelland & Stewart Inc., 1999.

Greenberg, N. Auden, W.H. and Kallman, C. eds. *An Elizabethan Song Book*, Faber & Faber 1968.

Gridley, Mark C. *Jazz Styles*. 6th ed. Prentice, 1997.

Griffin, Clive D. *Folk Music in Britain, Ireland and the USA (Music Matters)*. Batsford 1990.

Grout, Donald Jay and Palisca, Claude V. *A History of Western Music*, 6th ed., W.W. Norton & Co., 2000.

Guralnick, Peter, *Sweet Soul Music*. Bay Back Books, 1999.

Hadlock, Richard. *Jazz Masters of the Twenties*. Da Capo, 1986.

Hakim, Joy. *War, Peace, and All That Jazz 1918-1945*. Oxford University Press, 3rd edition, 2002.

Hamilton, Virginia. *Many Thousand Gone: African Americans from Slavery to Freedom*. Knopf, 1993.

Hamm, Charles. *Yesterdays: Popular Song in America*. Norton, 1979.

Hardy, Phil, and David Laing. *Encyclopedia of Rock*. Schirmer, 1987.

Harris, Lesley Ellen. *Canadian Copyright Law*. McGraw-Hill Ryerson, Toronto, Canada.

Harrison, D. D., *Black Pearls: Blues Queens of the 1920s*. Rutgers University Press, 1990.

Harrison, Tom. *Popular Music*. Canadian 2000 National Edition, McClelland & Stewart Inc., 1999.

Harvard University Libraries and Research Centers. Cambridge, Massachusetts, USA.

Heilbroner, R.L., & Singer, A., *The Economic Transformation of America: 1600 to Present*, 2d ed. 1984.

Hennessey, Thomas. *From Jazz to Swing: African-American Jazz Musicians and Their Music, 1890-1935*. Wayne State University Press, 1994.

Hentoff, Nat. *Listen to the Stories: Nat Hentoff on Jazz and Country Music*. Da Capo Press, 2000.

Hill, Daniel G. *The Freedom Seekers, Blacks in Early Canada*. Stoddart, 1992.

Hiller, J., and Neary, P., Eds. *Newfoundland in the Nineteenth and Twentieth Centuries*. 1980.

Hitchcock, H.W., Sadie S., eds. *New Grove Dictionary of American Music*. Grove's Dictionaries, 1986.

Hodeir, Andre, *Jazz: Its Evolution and essence*. Da Capo 1975; *Towards Jazz*, Da Capo 1976.

Hoppin, Richard H. *Medieval Music*. W.W. Norton & Company, 1978.

Hornsby, Alton, and Straub, D. G. *African American Chronology*. 2 vols. Gale Research, 1993.

Horstman, Dorothy. *Sing Your Heart Out, Country Boy*, rev. ed. Country Music Foundation Press, 1986.

International Photo & Images Copyright Clearances of New York. New York City, NY, USA.

Inukshuk Records, The Inuit Artist World Show Case, 1996; Katutjatut Throat Singing by Alacie Tullaugaq

& Lucy Amarualik, 1998; Nunavik Concert, 1993; Tradition, 2001; Inukshuk Productions.

Jackson, J. A., *Big Beat Heat: Alan Freed and the Early Years of Rock and Roll*. Schirmer Books, 2000; *American Bandstand: Dick Clark and the Making of a Rock'n'Roll Empire*. Oxford Univ. Pr, 1997.

John Abbott College, Music Program. Ste. Anne de Bellevue, Quebec, Canada.

Josephson, Matthew. *Edison: A Biography*. John Wiley & Sons, 1992.

Kamin, Jonathan L. The White R&B Audience and the Music Industry, 1952–1956, Popular Music and Society 4: 170–187, 1974; Rhythm & Blues in White America: Rock and Roll as Acculturation and Perceptual Learning. Dissertation Abstracts International 37 (Sept. 1986): 1805-06A; *Taking the roll out of rock 'n' roll. Reverse acculturation*. In: Popular Music And Society, Fall 1972, II, 1-17, 1972.

Karpeles, Maud, *An Introduction to English Folk Song*. Oxford University Press, 1987.

Kein, Sybil ed. *Creole: The History and Legacy of Louisiana's Free People of Color*. Louisiana Pr., 2000.

Kernfeld, Barry, ed. *The New Grove Dictionary of Jazz*. Grove, 1994; *What to Listen for in Jazz*. 1995.

Kingsbury P. ed. *The Encyclopedia of Country Music: The Ultimate Guide to the Music*. Oxford Pr, 1998.

Kohanov, Linda. *All Music Guide: New Age*. 1992 - 2003 AEC One Stop Group, Inc.

Kolchin, Peter. *American Slavery, 1619-1877*. Hill & Wang, 1993.

L. Harrison, Frank. *Music in Medieval Britain*. 1958.

Larkin, C. ed. *The Guinness Encyclopedia of Popular Music*. 6 vol. Grove's Dictionaries, Stockton, 1995.

Laufenberg, Cindy, ed. *Songwriter's Market*. Writer's Digest, 1996.

Le Huray, Peter. *Music and the Reformation in England, 1549-1660*, 1967.

Lees, Gene and Reeves, John. *Jazz Lives*. McClelland & Stewart, 1992.

Lehr, G. *Come and I Will Sing to You: A Newfoundland Song Book*. 1985;

Leonard, David P. *"The Canadian Music Industry"*, *The Music Business Handbook & Career Guide, 4th & 5th editions* by David Baskerville. Sage Publications.

Libin, Laurence. *American Musical Instruments in the Metropolitan Museum of Art*. Norton, 1985.

Library of Congress. Washington D.C. Archive of Folk Culture Collections.

Library of Parliament. Ottawa, Canada.

Ling, Jan, *A History of European Folk Music*, trans. by L. and R. Schenck. 1997.

Lissauer, Robert. *Lissauer's Encyclopedia of Popular Music in America, 1888 to the Present*. 3 vol. Rev. ed. Facts On File, 1996.

Litchfield, J. *The Canadian Jazz Discography 1916-1980*. University of Toronto Press, 1983.

Litwack, Leon F. *North of Slavery: The Negro in the Free States, 1790-1860*. 1961, reprinted 1970; Eds. with Meier, August. Black Leaders of the Nineteenth Century. University of Illinois Press, 1988.

Litweiler, John. The Freedom Principle, Jazz After 1958'. (Da Capo, 1989).

Lomax, Alan *The Land Where Blues Began*. 1993; *The Folk Songs of North America*. Doubleday, 1975; *Folk Song Style and Culture*. 1978; with John Lomax, *Cowboy Songs and Other Frontier Ballads*. Schirmer Books, 1986; *Adventures of a Ballad*. Hunter Macmillan Pub Co 1971.

Longyear, R. M. *19th-century Romanticism in Music*, 3rd ed. 1988. Prentice Hall History of Music Series.

Lornell, Kip, *Introducing American Folk Music*. McGraw-Hill Humanities, 1993.

Lovett, Bobby L. *The African-American History of Nashville, Tennessee, 1780-1930: Elites and Dilemmas*. University of Arkansas Press, 1999.

Lower, Arthur R.M. *Colony to Nation*. Toronto: McClelland and Stewart Ltd., 1977.

Lupher, Antonio. *Civil War Music*, A. Lupher, 1999-2000.

Mackaay & Gendreau. *Canadian Legislation on Intellectual Property*. Carswell Publishing.

MacNutt, W. S., *New Brunswick: A History, 1784-1867*. 1963; *New Brunswick and Its People*. 1966; *The Atlantic Provinces: The Emergence of Colonial Society, 1712-1857*. 1965.

Malcomson, Scott. *One Drop of Blood: The American Misadventure of Race*. Farrar, Straus-Giroux, 2000.

Malone, Bill C., *Country Music, U.S.A.*, 2nd ed. Univ. of Texas Press, 1985.

Manuel, P. L.. *Popular Musics of the Non-Western World: An Introductory Survey*. Oxford Univ Pr, 1990.

Marcus, G., *Mystery Train: Images of America in Rock and Roll Music*, Plume 4th ed. 1997.

Marsalis, W. & Hasse, J.E. *Beyond Category: The Life & Genius of Duke Ellington*. DaCapo Press, 1995.

Mason, Michael, ed., *The Country Music Book*. Scribner, 1985.

Matthiessen, Maria Von, *Songs from the Hills: An Intimate Look at Country Music*. Diane Pub. Co., 1993.

McAleer, Dave. *The All Music Book of Hit Singles*. Miller Freeman, 1994.

McCloud, B. *Definitive Country: Ultimate Encyclopedia of Country Music & Performers*. Berkley, 1995.

McCutcheon, Lynn E.; *Rhythm and Blues*. Rw Beatty, 1971.

McGill University Faculty of Music, Marvin Duchow Music Library, Montreal, Quebec, Canada.

McLeese, Don, *Popular Music*. Austin American-Statesman, Rolling Stone magazine, University of Iowa.

McNeil, Keith and Rusty. *Civil War Songs with historical narration*. WEM Records, 1989

McPherson, James M. *Battle Cry of Freedom*. Oxford University Press, 1988.

Mellers, Wilfred. *Music in a New Found Land*. Oxford Univ. Press, 1987)

Miller, Jim, ed. *The Rolling Stone Illustrated History of Rock & Roll*. Rolling Stone, 1992.

Miller, Mark. *Jazz in Canada: Fourteen Lives.* 1982; *Boogie, Pete & The Senator: Canadian Musicians in Jazz, the Eighties.* 1987; *Cool Blues: Charlie Parker in Canada, 1953.* 1989; *Such Melodious Racket: The Lost History of Jazz in Canada, 1914-1949.* 1997.

Miller, Philip L. *The Ring of Words: An Anthology of Song Texts,* ed. W.W. Norton & Company 1973.

Miller, Randall M., and Smith, J. D., eds. *Dictionary of Afro-American Slavery.* Greenwood, 1988; with Roger Boar *The Incredible Music Machine.* 1982.

Miller, Terry, *Folk Music in America: A Reference Guide.* Garland Publishing, 1987.

Mississippi Department of Archives and History.

Mississippi Valley Collection, Memphis State University.

Montreal Archives. Montreal, Quebec, Canada.

Morgan, Robert P. *Anthology of Twentieth-century Music.* W.W. Norton, 1992.

Morrison, Craig. *Go Cat Go! Rockabilly Music and Its Makers.* University of Illinois Press, 1996.

Morrison, Samuel E. *The Oxford History of the American People,* Vol. 2, N.Y.: Oxford University Press, 1972; with Commager, H. S., *The Growth of the American Republic,* 2 vols., 7th ed. 1980.

Music Directory Canada. Norris Whitney Communications Publishing.

National Academy of Recording Arts & Sciences (NARAS), Grammy Awards. Santa Monica, California.

National Archives & Public Record Office of England, Wales, UK. Kew, Richmond, Surrey, UK.

National Archives of Canada. Ottawa, Ontario, Canada.

National Archives, Washington, D.C., USA.

National Assembly of Quebec. Quebec City, Quebec, Canada.

National Gallery of Canada. Ottawa, Ontario, Canada.

National Library of Canada. Ottawa, Ontario, Canada.

National Park Service. U.S. Department of the Interior, Washington, D.C. USA.

National Underground Railroad Freedom Center, Cincinnati, Ohio, USA.

National Underground Railroad Museum, Maysville, Kentucky, USA.

Nettl, Bruno, ed., *Folk and Traditional Music of the Western Continents,* Rev. and ed. by Valerie Woodring Goertzen. 3d ed. Prentice-Hall, 1990; *Excursions in World Music,* 2d ed. 1996; *The Study of Ethnomusicology, The Western Impact on World Music*; with Myers, Helen. *Folk Music in the United States, an Introduction,* 3rd ed. Wayne State Univ. Press, 1976.

New American Library, *Folk Song USA,* Reissue edition, June 1983; *American Ballads,* Dover Pub, November 1994; *Nashville: Music City USA.* Harry N. Abrams Pub. 1985.

New Oxford History of Music, 10 vol. (1954-90), various editors, Oxford University Press, 1995.

New York Public Library, New York City, NY, USA.

Newfoundland and Labrador Provincial Archives Division. St-John's, Newfoundland, Canada.

Nite, N. *Rock on Almanac: The First Four Decades of Rock 'N' Roll: A Chronology,* HarperCollins, 1989.

Norman, Philip. *The True Story of the Beatles.* Hamish Hamilton Ltd. 1981 London, UK.

North American Black Historical Museum. Amherstburg, Ontario, Canada.

Oliver, Paul. *Blues Fell This Morning: Meaning in the Blues.* 2d ed. Cambridge University Press, 1990.

Ontario Black History Society Archives. Toronto, Ontario, Canada.

Ontario Legislative Library. Toronto, Ontario, Canada.

Ouellet, F. *Lower Canada 1791-1840.* 1980; *Economic & Social History of Quebec, 1760-1850.* tr. 1980.

Oxford University Libraries and Research Centers. Oxford, UK.

Palisca, Claude V. *Baroque Music,* 3rd ed. 1991. The Prentice Hall History of Music Series;

Pamphlets and documentation published by SOCAN, CMRRA, ACTRA, AVLA, CIRPA, CARAS, SODRAC, SOPROQ, ADISQ, BMI, ASCAP, SESAC, SACEM.

Panassie, H., *The Real Jazz,* 1960; repr. 1973.

Pareles, Jon, editor. *The Rolling Stone Encyclopedia Of Rock & Roll.* Rolling Stone Press, 1983.

Parish, Peter J., *Slavery, History and Historians.* 1989.

Passman, Don. *All You Need To Know About The Music Business.* Simon & Schuster.

Pauly, Reinhard G. *Music in the Classic Period,* 3rd ed. 1988. The Prentice Hall History of Music Series.

Paymer, Marvin E., ed. *Facts Behind the Songs: A Handbook of American Popular Music from the Nineties to the '90s.* Garland, 1993.

Public Broadcasting System (PBS Television), *The American Experience: Stephen Foster,* WITF, Harrisburg, 2001; *American Roots Music,* Ginger Group Production, 2001; *Martine Scorsese Presents The Blues: A Musical Journey.* Vulcan/Road Movies Production, 2003; *All Day and All Night: Memories from Beale Street Musicians.* Center for Southern Folklore, 1990. *The American Experience: Muddy Waters Can't Be Satisfied,* Temolo Productions, 2003; *Straight Shooter: The Story of the Mamas & the Papas,* Hallway Group Productions, 1988; *Preservation Hall Jazz Band: A Night in New Orleans, Johnny Cash Anthology,* Hallyway Entertainment & Distribution; Independent Lens: *Make 'Em Dance: The Hackberry Ramblers' Story,* Fretless Pictures, 2000; *Frame After Frame: The Images of Herman Leonard,* Louisiana Educational TV Authority, 1997;

205

Peacock, K. *Songs of the Newfoundland Outports.* 3 vols, 1965.

Pen, Ronald. Introduction To Music. McGraw-Hill Trade 1991; with Jean Ritchie, Alan Lomax, Folk Songs of the Southern Appalachians. University Press of Kentucky; 2nd edition, 1997.

Podell, Janet, ed., *Rock Music in America.* H.W. Wilson, 1987.

Porter, Lewis. *Jazz: A Century of Change.* Wadsworth Pub. 1997; with Michael Ullman & Edward Hazell, *Jazz: From its Origins to the Present.* Prentice Hall 1992.

Prawer, S.S., ed. *The Penguin Book of Lieder.* Penguin Publishing, 1987.

Previn, Andre. *Andre Previn's Guide to the Orchestra.* Putnam, 1983.

Prince Edward Island Public Archives and Records Office. Charlottetown, PEI, Canada.

Public Archives of Canada. Ottawa, Canada.

Public Archives of Nova Scotia. Halifax, Nova Scotia, Canada.

Purvis, Thomas L. *A Dictionary of American History.* Blackwell, 1995.

Randel, Don Michael (ed.), *The New Harvard Dictionary of Music.* 1986.

Read, Oliver and Welch, Walter L. *From Tin Foil to Stereo* (phonographic history), 2nd ed. 1976.

Rees, Dafydd, and Luke Crampton. *Rock Movers and Shakers.* Rev. ed. ABC-CLIO, 1991.

Reese, Gustave. *Music in the Renaissance,* rev. ed. 1959.

Remnant, M. *Musical Instruments: An Illustrated History: From Antiquity to the Present.* Amadeus, 1990.

Richards, Laura E., and Elliott, Maud Howe. *Julia Ward Howe, 1819-1910.* Cherokee Pub. Co., 1990.

Richards, Tad, and Shestack, Melvin, *The New Country Music Encyclopedia* (1993).

Riethmüller, Albrecht and Zaminer, Frieder, eds., *Die Musik des Altertums,* 1989.

Ro, Ronin, Have Gun Will Travel: The Spectacular Rise and Violent Fall of Death Row Records, 1998.

Robinson, Deanna C. *Music at the Margins: Popular Music and Global Cultural Diversity.* Sage, 1991.

Rogers, Al. *Amazing Grace: The Story of John Newton.* July-August 1996 issue of *"Away Here in Texas".*

Romanowski, P., & George-Warren, H., eds., *The New Rolling Stone Encyclopedia of Rock n Roll.* 1995.

Root, Deane L. *American Popular Stage Music, 1860-1880.* Umi Research Pr., 1981; editor, *Resources of American Music History: A Directory of Source Materials from Colonial Times to World War II.* Univ. of Illinois Pr., 1981; with Saunders, Steven. *The Music of Stephen C. Foster: 1844-1855: 1856 1869: A Critical Edition.* Smithsonian Institution Press, 1990.

Ryback, Timothy W. *Rock Around the Bloc: A History of Rock Music in Eastern Europe and the Soviet Union.* Oxford University Press, 1990.

Ryerson, Stanley B., *Unequal Union: Confederation and the Roots of Conflict in the Canadas, 1815-1873,* 1968; *The Founding of Canada: Beginnings to 1815.* Progress Books, 1975.

Sadie, Stanley, ed., *The New Grove Dictionary of Music and Musicians,* 20 vols. 1980, repr. 1993, 3 vols. Macmillan, London, 1984; *Norton-Grove Concise Encyclopedia of Music.* Rev. ed. Norton, 1994.

Salzman, Eric. *Twentieth-century Music,* 3rd ed. 1988 The Prentice Hall History of Music Series.

Sandberg, L. and Weissman, D., *The Folk Music Sourcebook,* Da Capo rev. ed. 1990.

Sanderson, Paul. *Musicians & the Law in Canada.* Carswell Publishing.

Sauvé, Paulette. *Le compositeur Calixa Lavallée.* Musée régional de Calixa Lavallée. 310, rang de la Beauce, Calixa-Lavallée, Québec, J0L 1A0.

Scheurer, T. E., ed., *American Popular Music: The Age of Rock, Vol. 2* Popular Press, 1990.

Schofield, Carey. Jagger. Methuen London, 1983.

Schuller, Gunther. *Early Jazz: Its Roots and Musical Development.* Oxford University Press, 1968, 1986; *The Swing Era: The Development of Jazz, 1930-1945.* Oxford University Press, 1989.

Schwartz, Daylle. *Start and Run Your Own Record Label.* Watson-Guptill Publishing.

Seeger, R.C. American Folk Songs for Children. Doubleday, 1980.

Shaw, Arnold. *The Jazz Age: Popular Music of the 1920's.* American Philological Ass. 1987; *Honkers & Shouters: The Rhythm & Blues Years.* MacMillan Pub Co., Repr. ed. 1986; *The Rockin' 50's,* 1987.

Shemel & Krasilovsky. *This Business of Music.* Watson-Guptill Publishing; *More About This Business of Music.* Billboard Books.

Siebert, William H., *Underground Railroad from Slavery to Freedom.* NY, 1898; repr. 1968.

Silverman, Jerry. *Ballads & Songs of the Civil War.* Mel Bay Publications, Inc., Pacific, MO, 1993.

Slonimsky, Nicolas *Music Since 1900,* 5th ed.(1994.

Smith, Leonard H., *Nova Scotia Immigrants to 1867.* 1994.

Sonnier, Austin Jr, *A Guide to the Blues: History's Who's Who, Research Sources.* Greenwood, 1994.

Spencer, Peter. *World Beat: A Listener's Guide to Contemporary World Music on CD.* A Cappella, 1992.

Stambler, Irwin, and Landon, Grelun. *The Encyclopedia of Folk, Country, & Western Music.* 2nd ed. St. Martin's, 1983; *The Encyclopedia of Pop, Rock and Soul.* Rev. ed. St. Martin's, 1989; *Country Music: The Encyclopedia.* Griffin Trade Paperback, 2000.

Statistics Canada Library, Ottawa, Ontario Canada.

Stevens, Denis, ed., *A History of Song,* Greenwood Publishing, 1982.

Stokes, W. R. *The Jazz Scene: An Informal History from New Orleans to 1990.* Oxford Univ. Press, 1991.

Stolba, K Marie *The Development of Western Music: A History*, 2nd ed. Brown & Benchmark, 1994.

Sudhalter, Richard M., *Bix: Man and Legend* (Leon Bix Beiderbecke), Crown Publishing Group, 1974; *Lost Chords: White Musicians and Their Contribution to Jazz, 1915-1945*. Oxford Univ. Pr., 2001; *Stardust Melody: The Life and Music of Hoagy Carmichael*, Oxford Univ. Press, 2003; with Elliott, Susan, Kimball, Robert. *You're the Top: Cole Porter in the 1930s*. Indiana Historical Society, 1992.

Sweet, Walter. *Complete Music for Fife & Drum*. Mel Bay Publications, Inc., Pacific, MO, 1996.

Taraborrelli, J. Randy. *Michael Jackson: The Magic and the Madness*. Carol Publishing Group, 1991.

Television Networks: A&E - *Dizzy Gillespie*, Gene Davis Group, 2001; True Channel - *John Lee Hooker: That's My Story*, Kick Production, 2000; CBS - 60 Minutes segment: *King* Solomon Burke, 2003; TVA-Musicographie: *Zachary Richard/Richard Séguin* TV Maxplus Productions, 2002; VH1-Ultimate Albums: *Eminem, The Marshall Mathers LP*, 2002 & *Run-DMC, Raising Hell*, 2002.

Temperley, Nicholas. *The Music of the English Parish Church*, 2 vol. 1979.

Terkel, Studs. *Giants of Jazz*, rev. ed. Harper, 1975; *Voices of our Time: Five Decades of Studs Terkel Interviews*. Audiocassettes, Highbridge Company.

Tharp, Louise Hall, *Three Saints and a Sinner: Julia Ward Howe, Louisa, Annie, and Sam Ward*. 1956.

Thomas, H. *The Slave Trade: The Story of the Atlantic Slave Trade; 1440-1870*. Simon&Schuster, 1997.

Thomas, Phil J. *Songs of the Pacific Northwest*. Hancock House Publishers, 1980.

Tichi, Cecelia, *High Lonesome: The American Culture of Country Music*. Univ. North Carolina Pr, 1994.

Tirro, Frank. *Jazz: A History*. 2nd ed. Norton, 1993.

Titon, Jeff Todd, ed et al. *Worlds of Music: An Introduction to the Music of the World's Peoples*. Schirmer Books, 4th ed., 2001.

Toronto Public Library. Toronto, Ontario, Canada.

Tosches, N. *Unsung Heroes of R'N'R: The Birth of Rock in the Wild Years Before Elvis*. DaCapo Pr 1999.

Trebas Institute, Media Design & Technology College, Music Business Administration Program. Toronto, Ontario & Montreal, Quebec, Canada. David P. Leonard, President, CEO, founder.

Trynka, Paul, ed. *Rock Hardware*. (History of rock instruments) Miller Freeman, 1997.

Tucker, Mark, *Ellington: The Early Years* (Music in American Life Series). University Illinois Pr, 1991.

UCLA Libraries and Museums, Los Angeles, California, USA.

Underground Railroad Museum, Flushing, Ohio, USA.

Underground Railroad Network, African-Canadian Heritage Tour. Chatham, Ontario.

United States Census Bureau, Washington DC, USA.

University of Missouri-Kansas City Archives, Kansas City, Missouri, USA.

Vanier College, Music Industry Seminars & Audio Recording Technology Program. 815 Ste-Croix Avenue, Saint-Laurent, Quebec, Canada.

Vinet, Mark. *Canada and the American Civil War: Prelude To War.* 2001 Wadem Publishing, 117 Bellevue street, Vaudreuil-sur-le-Lac, Quebec, Canada, J7V-8P3. Tel: 450-510-1102 / 450-371-1803. Fax: 450-510-1095. mark@markvinet.com www.markvinet.com ; *Le Québec/Canada et la Guerre de Sécession américaine, 1861-1865*. Éditions Wadem, 2002.

Wade, Mason. *The French Canadians, 1760-1967*, 2 vols. Macmillan, 1968.

Ward, E., et al., *Rock of Age: The Rolling Stone History of Rock and Roll*. Simon & Schuster 1987.

Waterman, Christopher Alan. *Juju: A Social History and Ethnography of an African Popular Music (Chicago Studies in Ethnomusicology)*. University of Chicago Press 1990; with Larry Starr, *American Popular Music: From Minstrelsy to MTV*, Oxford University Press; Book & CD ed., 2002.

Waters, Ethel, et al. *His Eye Is on the Sparrow: An Autobiography*. Da Capo Press, Reprint 2000.

Westbrook, Alonzo. *Hip Hoptionary TM : The Dictionary of Hip Hop Terminology*. Harlem Moon, 2002.

Westrup, Jack A. *The New Oxford History of Music*. Oxford University Press, 1991.

Whitburn, Joel. *Billboard Top One Thousand Singles 1955-1986*. Hal Leonard, 1986.

White, A. & Bronson, F. *The Billboard Book of Number One Rhythm and Blues Hits*. Billboard Bks, 1993.

White, T. *Music to My Ears: The Billboard Essays: Profiles of Popular Music in the '90s*. Holt, 1996.

Wicke, Peter. *Rock Music: Culture, Aesthetics and Sociology*. Cambridge University Press, 1990.

Wilder, Alec. *American Popular Song: The Great Innovators, 1900-1950*. Oxford Univ. Press, 1990.

Wile, Frederic W. *Emile Berliner: Maker of the Microphone*. Ayer Publishing 1926, reprinted 1974.

Williams, M. *The Jazz Tradition*, MacMillan, 1993; *Jazz Master of New Orleans*, MacMillan, 1967.

Wilmer, Valerie. As Serious as Your Life. Chicago Review, 1980.

Wolff, Francis, et al. *The Blue Note Years: The Jazz Photography of Francis Wolff*. (Alfred Lion) Rizzoli, 2001; *Blue Note: A History of Modern Jazz*, (film) Emd/Blue Note, 1996.

World Bk.; McClelland and Stewart; Funk & Wagnalls; Microsoft; Learning Company; Grolier; Britannica; Broderbund, Interactive multimedia.

Wynn, Ron, ed. et al. *All Music Guide to Jazz: The Best CD's, Albums & Tapes*. Miller Freeman, 1994.

Yudkin, Jeremy *Music in Medieval Europe*. The Prentice Hall History of Music Series, 1989.

clockwise from top left: April Wine, The Cars,
Yes, Boston, Journey, Van Halen

Eric Clapton

Kiss

INDEX